MANAGEMENT
GREED, FEAR, LOATHING, RESPONSIBILITY,
MATERIALISM
AND
THE AMERICAN DREAM

ERNIE SCHULTZE

ISBN-13: 978-0615870991 (SWPUBL Publishing)

ISBN-10: 0615870996

CONTENTS

INTRODUCTION

When we think of the world of business, we picture what our own interaction would be with that business or company. When we go to a movie, our experience with the person at the ticket booth influences our judgment of the movie house itself. Even at the dentist's office, the receptionist, the décor in the waiting lobby, the date on the magazines and the dentist's attitude, all factors when deciding if we'll be a returning client or not.

Let's say we need financial services. We have worked hard to put money aside for our retirement yet lack knowledge of how to invest so we feel we need help. It is important to find an investment advisor or manager with expertise, but it is paramount to find a professional with integrity who you can trust. You need someone who does not have a secret agenda to take your money from you. This presents itself as a tough proposition, for many of us know that when it comes to money - especially large amounts of money - people will do anything to get that money if the opportunity presents itself. As the financial client, you perform your due diligence and try to uncover all possible evidence as to the extent of the financial professional's honesty. And we want to know that they really do know how to make us more money with the money we hand over to them.

When planning for our financial stability, it is only natural to compare several financial professionals through face-to-face meetings to smell them out. We look into their eyes when they talk to us; we scan the office walls for some kind of certificate and ask for references (even if they might be the professional's aunt and uncle). We check them out on Google to see if they have any lawsuits against them and ask the Financial Industry Regulatory Authority (FINRA) if they have any marks against their work. Do their letters or brochures contain bad grammar or typos?

It all seems fool proof.. until we discover that our professional has been swindling our hard-earned money right under our nose. And if our professional has been handing our money to another "professional" for a fee, we may have been ripped off legitimately, but ripped off nevertheless. If our professional is sending our money to a mutual fund manager, then that mutual fund manager is taking his share of our money without our knowledge. An entire chain of professionals may be taking our money while we go to sleep each night believing that our professional money manager has our best interests at heart rather than paying off his new Mercedes SL.

It is not until we read in the newspaper that our professional is running a Ponzi scheme that we become aware of any wrongdoing. Alternatively, maybe we hire another financial expert who turns to us on his chair and says, "They are taking your money and you are being ripped." Your first reaction is denial, which gradually grows into sadness upon the realization that you can perform all your due diligence and still have your money stolen from you. Even worse, the professional has stolen it from you in a way that you do not even realize. It is very common in the financial industry to die without ever becoming aware that your professional has taken huge amounts of your estate. An actual case of this is discussed later in this book.

There are, of course, levels of belief in a company, service or product. It does not matter much if a hamburger is not as tasty as you would like but you pay and forget it. The only reminder is if you develop a bellyache or worse, diarrhea, thanks to that morsel. This is something we have all gone through and we do not complain to the restaurant, even if we should. However, some products and services require our attention and we cannot let it go should there be a problem. It is a matter of degree.

When you go to a doctor, you expect to see medical degrees and hope to see special awards for their expertise in the field for which you came. Yet we hear news stories of doctors who are not really doctors, taking money from people until they are discovered to be fraudulent. There are news stories about lawyers who are not really lawyers, practicing law for years. What must be realized is that not all of the fraudulent practice in the professions is *ever found out.*

With so many fraudulent practices throughout these professions, how do we know whom to trust? This depends on how much we care about what they offer us and it depends on how much is expected of them. Anyone can call himself or she a financial manager with little or no background in finance and in most states there is no certificate or diploma required.

Much of what we are talking about in this writing comes from being on the outside of the company as consumers. However, do we realize these things when we are on the inside? Have you worked for a company and thought things were not quite right? What do I mean by all this?

-Management -

A company is always portending to be a management system. Management is the holy grail of any business school and a great concern within corporate culture. People sit in big offices wearing suits and collecting big paychecks all in the name of "management." Is this just a concept or does it somehow exist in some inherent structure? Management within a company is little more than a belief system. Approaches to management have been talked about for many years. There is the big boss CEO and the vice president reporting to the big boss CEO and the director reporting to the vice president and so on down the line. A company can downsize and cut middle management and customers may not even notice. Management is a concept perpetuated by language and belief. Add to that the threat of handing a check or not handing a check to those in the levels below the big boss and that is the glue for our concept of management.

This book contains real stories about real business situations. It is intended to give insight to the reader that many elements go into the existence, success or failure, longevity, health and quality of any company that can only be learned from real life.

No study on the differences between leadership and management, no account or case histories of famous companies, can explain how to run a company. What we have in academia are approaches and strategy models for running a company, and records of accomplishment for how they do and do not work. None of that tells you how to run a company.

The person running the company must have the ability to see the big picture. The bigger the company, the bigger this ability must be. This person must be able to sense the appeal of their product or service to the people that will buy it. They must be able to sense the amount of money made and how that money is used in order to continue the success of the company. There must be an understanding and an ability to adjust, through people, how departments interact and complement one another. Without this business sense, the company usually dies... but not always. There are small companies run by people who really do not understand how it all works. Regardless, the company makes a profit. These are managers who have found (sometimes by accident) employees who are able to make enough of a difference in how things are done to keep it all together.

Management is often referred to as a science. Business management, law, human resources, marketing, the study of unions and so many other subjects are nothing more than social psychology at work. Management is the study of human interaction. It is therefore paramount that the student of management begins by studying how and why people do what they do and understanding the consequences. Consequences are the great bugaboo for the manager, as they are sometimes the result of poorly made choices. Those results are hardly ever predictable, but when they turn out well, the manager gets credit. As an employee of both small and large companies and as the owner of my own firm involved in the inner workings of clients I have seen it all. I am always astounded by people in high places; how they work and what effect they have on the company overall in terms of employees and success of the business. This book is about how companies project a legitimate, profitable image even if they are not. It is about how customers perceive these images, and how these companies are managed and not managed from the inside.

Chapter One

Growing up I listened to all the ranting and raving about how horrible the world of business is by my father and brother. I understood the world of money as something one should not pursue; as if money would somehow take care of itself. Maybe it would fall from the sky, roll in with the tide or appear mysteriously in a bank account overnight. Early on, I understood that certain things were necessary in life, like food, clothing, electricity and a roof over one's head.

This view of life conflicted with the ultra-popular hippie view of the day. The consensus that from sex, drugs and rock and roll, a society would evolve where no one had to manufacture or produce anything and no one had to think to be a genius. Nor should there be a place where anyone should have to work to have all the goodies available to American life and the dream that goes with it. As the great guru of the '60s, Timothy Leary, famously put it, "tune in, turn on, and drop out." This quote referred to the horrors of earning a living in the material world. No one questioned where Leary got his fame and no one seemed to know where he got the fortune enabling him to live so well while he dropped LSD and spread the word of hippydom in the world of love. Being a tenured Harvard professor had its advantages. Indeed! Living in the woods and pooping in a hole in the dirt was thought to be far superior to working for the world of business where desperation, greed, materialism, evil and war were all part of the package.

Now you may not think I am going anywhere with this rant,

but I am. I am going to describe my experience of this world of desperation, greed and materialism as one who entered into it for the money, to connect with the female species, and for the associated status. It turned out that the pursuit of the female species was not so different to that of the pursuit of the world of business and desperation, greed and materialism. That, however, is a point of debate for psychologists. Let us explore my entrance to that world of horror, that world of business.

The Startup

After graduating from college, I understood the need to make big bucks if I was to sing the siren of the wealthy man to all the beautiful damsels waiting in the world. I had to find a way to make the dollars necessary to live the American dream. I had always heard the way to the top was by starting at the bottom, so I found a job at the bottom of a startup racquetball manufacturer. I was lucky enough to find a startup by a brilliant inventor. The company was spread out through a series of open commercial offices-made-production-facility in what was supposed to be an office complex. Whenever a company moved out of the complex, my company would rent the space and expand operations into the space left by it.

I had no idea how lucky I was. Starting work in a big company with little or no opportunity to adjust procedures or be creative would have been the end of that world for me. But this little startup demanded forward thinking, creative attitudes and an ability to see around the corner where no one had been before.

At first my job consisted of pulling orders from a public retailer off a warehouse shelf, gathering the products needed to fill the order, then boxing them up to be sent to whomever paid for the products. I did this tedious task each day, all the while visualizing myself ending up at the top of the ladder as chairman of the board or president of the company, commanding all the money a man could possibly stand. It was the only way I could justify doing this kind of work with my fresh M.A. and law degree. It was a way of "paying my dues."

This was a garage-style startup company. The founder surmised that the world was ready for a new kind of racquetball racquet. Until then, racquetball racquets were made of wood. The owner thought it would make for a better game if the racquet were made of aluminum and he was not wrong. When I started at this company, we sold about $20,000 worth of racquets the first year. Within three years, we had sold $12,000,000 worth of racquets.

This was an improvement to an existing product, much like the Apple Inc. products. The cell phone becomes the iPhone, the notebook becomes the iPad and so on. Truly new and revolutionary products are hard to sell to an unknowing market. It took many years to convince business owners to trust the computer rather than their trusty accounting ledger made of paper. The personal computer put many typewriters and many typists out of business and surprisingly it took a while. It was a revolutionary product and tough to sell. It is no big deal to sell markets on an evolutionary product like a metal, rather than a wood racquet.

Having said that, I think it is often hard to come up with an improvement on an existing product that is accepted by markets. Products like the computer have made their way into markets that were satisfied with the accountant with the ledger and typewriter. Yet the cell phone took years to become accepted. After all, who wanted to carry a damn leash around with them to be summoned by any party with another phone? The days of the endless rings when calling someone went out with technology of the "answering machine" and later, voice mail.

After a few months and some company growth, my first promotion came as assistant manager. With this new responsibility came a $.50 per hour raise. My manager went on vacation for a couple weeks, leaving me in charge. I spent that time working my way into the company network by answering the office telephone. People all over the company would call and be surprised by the new voice on the line. In this way, I developed relationships with people in key positions all around the company. I did my best to be professional and that meant being congenial, efficient, intelligent and worthy of their respect. When my manager returned, people asked for me and that created a bit of turbulence between us. I concentrated on the people in marketing and it was not long before I broke off from my original department and was given my own as Marketing Special Projects Coordinator with a set of my own handpicked people. I was on my way as I realized this would never have happened in a General Motors or a Bank of America. I was grateful, loyal and proud of my company.

This kind of thing could only happen in a highly successful startup situation. The mature company structure with all of its areas of operation already in place would never allow a new department to develop as it did for me. In a company like General Motors the thought of creating a new department would be perceived by management as a serious collapse of the normal. People would freak out until the idea died on the vine.

But at this racquetball manufacturing company, key people began to come visit me, take me to lunch and invite me out. The company was spread out all over town by now. We rented space wherever we could find it for our rapidly expanding company. Telephones were the only source of communication and many relationships were only known as a voice rather than by face-to-face meetings. I knew I had it made though, when people around the company started calling me and asking me what they should do and how to proceed in matters of marketing and operations. I was becoming indispensible in my own mind. If I were not there, how could the company continue to run? My manager informed me that my name had been coming up in board of directors meetings as the "go-to" guy in the company. I was lucky to have a manager who did not claim my ideas and actions as his own, who was comfortable with himself and his own work. It helps to a huge degree to have a mentor whose head is on straight. He had his own competence and when we met, the conversation was easy, energetic, productive and sometimes personal. It was not tense and bogus as these managerial relationships often are in a less capable company.

The money was rolling in and we were on top of it all. We were growing as a company in waves and the energy level was incredible. It was not long before the president announced that the company would build its own new building.

When people on the outside learned where I worked there was

always very positive feedback about the products and the company as well as for the game itself. Racquetball was a hot subject, a hugely popular game, and we were the kings. We even published the rules of the game for use in professional tournaments. Like all rules, we made them up to satisfy our marketing agenda.

After playing all the corporate games and becoming the superstar of the corporation, I found myself propelling to the top. As the pride and joy of the company, I was chosen to pick up the local winner of the beauty contest, who would accompany me to a shovel ceremony for our new facility. The days of moving into someone else's office space were over. The pageant winner and I drove to the site where we were to turn the dirt in front of the media and smile for the cameras; me standing proudly with my young date beside the president, CEO and board of directors. We handled our own press by supplying fact sheets to the invited television and newspapers reporters during these events. Fact sheets that showed what a grand company we were. That was my first lesson in public relations.

The president and founder of the company was no slacker. He had won several Olympic gold medals for the Javelin. He had sold the rights to a stringing machine he had invented, which gave him the capital to start this new company. He was also a preacher for several years and championed civil rights among other humane causes. He started many organizations with a cause such as the Big Brother/Big Sister Foundation. On top of all of this, he was an engineer.

Maybe it was his belief in civil rights, the sanctity of mankind, or the fact that he was a minimalist that he refused to show his wealth. Instead, he lived in a modest house and drove an old Volvo with bad paint. I joked with him about the Volvo, so he had it repainted at a quickie paint shop for $100 and bragged about it. He always wore a flannel shirt and looked like he had just gotten out of bed, sleeping in his clothes.

Recently, at 85 years old, he won the pole vault competition in the local Master's track meet. A very talented person indeed. He used to tell me he was embarrassed to show his wealth and was under the belief that people who needed to look wealthy suffered from low self-esteem. He thought the important objectives in life were the quality of the contributions you leave to your community rather than the size of your estate. Some of that got through to me. I was still working on the estate part.

He groomed me for his slot in the company and was quite up-front about it, much to the chagrin of my peers. All was going well and I was on my way with visions of stardom, riches and becoming a figure that lesser men would worship someday.

As luck would have it, a nasty recession came along with a vengeance and no one wanted to buy our products anymore. Turns out that Racquetball was a luxury, who knew? The orders dried up and it was every man for himself in the company. It is common for upper management to act aggressively, but when it comes to laying people off, they turn into wimps... My company hired a consultant from some unknown company in Canada to do their dirty work. He was born in the UK, and told stories of Hitler's bombs dropping when he was a child. It turned out he was much too young for this to have been true, a definite red flag. We knew this guy hated people and loved to fire them. He was a predator and deceptive. He acted as though he wanted to be your friend while looking for ways to split open your abdomen and let your guts spill out where he could stomp on them as they slid over the tops of your shoes. He did the devil's work and everyone in the company knew it, even though there was the pretense of normalcy throughout the company. The English accent gave him an aura of sophistication, decency and class where there was none.

My first clue should have been the firing of 50 people from the production floor. Hell, I did not know there were more than 10 down there. These were the little people in the corporate belly and had little or nothing to do with my stature there. After all, I was president of the American Management Association and gave speeches to the employees. I was becoming delusional and in denial of my own mortality.

All the while, I was still thinking I was indispensable. Why I was given all the creative freedom one could be given in a company. I received an award for developing a partnership with a major beer company on a national racquetball tournament. This beer company paid us to coordinate a 30-city Racquetball event that would display their latest beer product. They launched a national advertising campaign for their product and tournament sponsorship. It was huge, celebrated throughout the country and received national news coverage in the sports media. I was touted as the company hero and a second coming of Christ at a major marketing event at the Hotel Del Coronado. All attendees were waiting breathlessly for my appearance and thoughts wherever I happened to show up at that great celebration of corporate greed, hype, materialism and of course, my glorious accomplishments.

Getting a tournament paid for by the largest beer company in the world was not an easy task. I had contacted the person who made the decision to hand us the money by finding his name – which was no easy task. That is, of course, always an important first step. I sent him a letter telling him how he could become a hero in the history of beer marketing by hooking up with the greatest and most popular sports product since the football. And he agreed. I hopped on a plane to St. Louis and met with he and his team at a meeting room filled with all types of beer trinkets and sports trophies. This was a perfect match and I proclaimed to this group of decision makers how racquetball was the next biggest sport to raise its athletic supporter to the level of this sponsor. The next trophy in that meeting room would come from the tournament they would pay for and my company would run it for them. The approval came before I left the building.

It was not easy getting into that room. I had called my decision maker at the beer company numerous times after writing numerous letters to him. My way in was through his secretary. To contact him I had to go through his secretary. I made a point to be totally professional and honest with her. We developed a telephone relationship and after a few tries, she volunteered to fish my letter out of the garbage and hand it to him. That was my foot in the door and the start of my aura as the wizard at getting big things done in my company.

I was asked to develop procedures, styles and realities concomitant of a business genius, with corporate beauties waiting to meet me in hopes of developing a corporately coveted relationship -- the up and comer who would someday be CEO of the company.

I was also the conduit to our advertising agency and they knew that their relationship with me meant millions of dollars to them in client services each month. It is the way with clients and agencies; one second there is millions in revenues and then there is none. They invited me to the company party each Friday, where I hobnobbed with the employees and my every utterance was sacred. Each Friday there was a 20-gallon barrel of margaritas and the fun went on into the night. At the end of the evening, one of the agency females would invite me to her home. Who was I to refuse such a complimentary gesture?

The ad and PR business looked good to me, and I thought I would do well to work in an agency, should I ever leave here. What I was not ready for was the president and founder coming to me and saying, "If you have ever thought of moving on and taking advantage of your position here in another company, now is the time."

What he, of course, was telling me is that I was on my way out, because the company was about to be sold to a large racket company in New Jersey. The racket company would give the best jobs, including mine, as a reward to their own people. The best-laid plans can go to hell in no time at all.

No matter how secure you may feel, no matter how loved you are and no matter what you have done to contribute to the survival or growth of the company, a pink slip is always three feet behind. Like death, it is waiting for the right moment to take you and you cannot turn around fast enough to see it because it dodges out of sight before you can make eye contact with it. But it is always there, waiting just the same.

One cannot help but be alarmed at the possibility of not having a check come to you each month. That could mean losing your house, your car, your dog to the animal shelter and eventually, finding your place among the homeless folks downtown. I was just not cut out for that and of course; the female species could not look past problems of that sort in a man.

Then one day it came. I was asked out for lunch by the newly hired corporate gun. From across the table he told me of the woes of the company and how a racket company in New Jersey was buying it and I had the option to quit or be laid off. My life of stardom flashed before my eyes as if I had died. I needed a second or two to recoup. Saying nothing, I reached for my hamburger, took a bite, and remained quiet while my lunch mate sat staring into my eyes, savoring the kill. I looked back at him after a loud swallow of burger and said in the most confident manner, "I quit."

My life of stardom was traded for unemployment after a huge goodbye party thrown by the company.

I walked out of that party alone, drove home and as I walked up the stairs to my house overlooking the beautiful pacific, I stubbed my toe on the steps. I broke the big toe on the right foot. It could have been an accident or it could have been a subconscious punishment of self, most likely the latter. No matter how little at fault you are at a moment like that, self-guilt and loathing is in the human DNA and it is something to be reckoned with on such an occasion.

I took time to lick my wounds. The unemployed life is a free life where I once again discovered the fun involved in doing what you want to do whenever you want to do it, as long as unemployment insurance footed the bill. The women on the beaches of southern California and the hippy influence made for a nice vacation from corporate life and responsibility.

As the end of this vacation loomed, I longed to do something to get back to the appearance of wealth and power. Like a normal business schmuck, I thought I had to work for a company already established, hoping to ride it like a train into the night of greed, fear, loathing, responsibility, materialism and of course, the American dream.

Chapter Two

Since I always loved what I saw in ad agency life, I thought I should join up with an ad or PR agency. I wanted an impressive title like Account Executive or Exalted Ruler. I needed a title impressive enough to draw the attention of females.

I found an advertising agency that was willing to take me seriously. It was founded by a rather ancient man from New York City who claimed to be an executive from the Gray Agency and half a dozen other major agencies from New York.

During my first and only interview with him, he was quite lucent and reasonable. Although a bit of a showman and braggart, he was pleasant and somewhat professional. He brought in his main man, Paul, a fellow who had a major penchant for vodka and a side business selling binders to corporations both locally and in Tijuana. Paul drove a spectacular 20-year-old Chrysler that had a slight misfire. Not only was he the agency's main man and a binder salesman, but he managed a Glen Miller type band in an old dive bar.

He had a very professional way about him and talked of his prior life as a sales person for IBM. How he had descended to this level could only be explained by his penchant for vodka. One day Paul asked me if I would go with him to Tijuana to sell some of his binders. This was before an American could cross the southern border and feel relatively assured they would come back alive. I agreed and we traveled to Tijuana.

Once in Mexico and parked, he directed me towards an old

building leading me inside to a receptionist's desk. She knew him
and he said a few words in Spanish to her, handing her a few black
binders. She took the binders and disappeared up some stairs.
Although nothing illegal was obviously transpiring, this was not
normal business protocol. We sat in the lobby for quite a long time,
maybe an hour or so. Paul looked content and seemed assured he
was going to make a sale. Sure enough, the receptionist came back
down the stairs with an array of orders for thousands of binders.
Everything about this trip seemed almost surreal.

We got back into his old Chrysler and headed for a local
Mexican restaurant. We had tacos and Paul had vodka. Then he
had vodka, and another. We got back into his car and headed for
our agency of record. He seemed sober but I had no idea what he
looked like drunk either. His system had to be pumping more
alcohol than blood. We arrived at the office, took the elevator to
the third floor, and separated into our adjacent offices. A few
minutes had passed when I heard a loud boom like ten sticks of
dynamite blowing at once. I ran into the hall and saw people
dashing into Paul's office. I followed and there was Paul, tipped
over backwards in his chair with the phone receiver lying next to
him. But that was not the least of it. He had removed all of his
clothes with the exception of his tie. So there he was in all his
splendor and glory, with his tie around his neck, lying on his back
in his chair while talking on the phone to someone as though
nothing were out of sync.

That was not to be the most unique experience here. The

agency founder and owner, Jack, was an endless source of entertainment. He vied for our attention, taking our focus away from our job. It did not seem as though he cared if we were doing our jobs or not. Jack could speak a good game but did not seem to have a full deck. He was around 75 years old if not older, but claimed he was pushing 50. This became the in-company joke.

Jack was short and skinny with a long dipping nose ending in a downward point. His eyebrows looked like mini toupees, dominating his face. He had no hair with the exception of the bald man's fringe around the side of his head. His droopy eyes were always red and you could see red veins running throughout his wrinkled face. Not a glamorous look for an ad agency executive.

There was something very wrong with the way he proceeded in the agency business, but who were we to question his sanity? As long as our payroll checks didn't bounce, we were fine.

I soon realized though, that he did not take himself, his business or any of his employees seriously. All he wanted was an audience who he had absolute command over. Whenever he had a personal issue, he called a meeting with the entire company.

He let his employees know in his own way that one has to rip people off to make money in business, talking of the naivety of those who were honest and ethical. More fear and loathing to deal with for sure on the part of an employee. Meanwhile, those of us in the company trying to earn a living by making his company viable became resentful of his frivolous meetings and business posture.

I was sure by now that he had no clue how to be professional in his demeanor, so how was it he had gotten here? He did not take it seriously, treating his business like a plaything. So where did he get the money to start this company if he wasn't a serious businessperson?

His shenanigans took valuable time from those of us who were trying to make something of his dismal agency. Getting him to listen to you was almost impossible. One time I devised a pseudo kidnap-ransom scheme just to submit him a request. I cut out letters from various magazines to spell out my request, pasted them onto letterhead and stuffed it into an envelope. The first note said, "Jack, please no more impromptu meetings." It helped for a while.

It became clear that he only wanted an advertising account if he could control it and perform his shenanigans for the new client. By asking subtle questions of those around me, I discovered his M.O. He would hire an account executive, and when the account executive brought in an account, he would take it over and manage it himself, firing the account executive. He could play Big Daddy and no longer have to pay that person. Pathetically, Jack had no problem taking another's hard gotten business. Especially at the expense of those creative enough to bring the account in.

If we had more than a few accounts, he would work his magic on them one at a time hyping and bull krapping his way through client meetings until they resigned. Meanwhile I was working on bringing them in quietly before he noticed.

I brought in an account for the most luxurious hotel in the

county. The manager was impressed with our portfolio Jack had pulled out a closet in his office, which no one had ever seen before. I took one of our writers and an artist as backup to the presentation for their advertising savvy and won the account after much massaging. Soon after I had reeled the account in, but before the contract had been signed, Jack found out and called the hotel's general manager to schedule lunch with their marketing people. I knew what would happen and it did. The old man would brag and make up crap about what a big shot he was and had single-handedly invented the Salk vaccine right after he ended WWII. There was little doubt we would lose the account before we could start managing it. About an hour after Jack returned from that lunch I got a call from the hotel and was told that they had chosen another agency. Apparently, they had second thoughts and did not think we could service the account properly.

As it turned out, Jack had bragged about how he had started a shoe store back east where all the shoes were one price. It turned out the manager of the hotel was familiar with the company, and asked Jack if he still owned the company. Jack whined like a child about how he had gotten sick and had to sell it. A silence fell over the meeting that screamed "Liar!" That was the end of his and our credibility after so much effort and preparation, sweat, tears and energy.

The company was depending on me to bring in new business without Jack finding out. I soon resigned myself to this as being a temporary situation in life.

Jack was clearly past the age of retirement. Dating himself by wearing a white fedora, never knowing quite what to do with it when we went to a client's offices for meetings. No one was wearing hats at that time; it was a cultural faux pas, so companies were ill prepared to deal with his appearance. He always looked around for somewhere to store his hat while we were meeting; after all, it is not polite to wear a hat indoors. Client offices never had a hat rack or even so much as a nail in the wall. He tried all kinds of ways to deal with it, often leaving it on a desk or a table by the receptionist or sometimes on a toilet lid in the men's bathroom. As he could not see past his cornea, quite often he would mistake the men's room for the women's. One time he had left the fedora in the women's restroom. There was no way we would get the account after he ambled into the women's restroom to retrieve his hat, with women yelling at him to get the hell out. Confused, he emerged as though it was all quite normal, clutching his white fedora in his trembling hand.

On another occasion, he took those of us he deemed most important to lunch at a fine hotel restaurant by the bay. Once again, he lamented that he was pushing 50 and we secretly grinned at each other. Then he began to brag about his new boat and invited us all to go for a ride on it after lunch. The way he talked about it the boat sounded like a yacht. I envisioned it with its own captain and living quarters. This was going to be a truly luxurious ride. The six of us went outside after lunch to a pier behind the hotel.

We passed multi-million dollar vessels before arriving at Jack's boat. It was maybe six feet long with four seats and no roof. We carefully stuffed ourselves into the boat from the side of the dock with each extra pound lowering the boat further into the water. The extra two people got in side by side in the rear seats. It was like a sardine can in there and the water line was dangerously close to the top railing with all the extra weight. He started the engine with much glee, backing away from the dock in slow motion because of the weight, engine full speed. Then he proceeded forward. We ever so slowly edged away from the dock. The faster we went, the more water slopped over the edge soaking us. He finally turned us around heading back to the dock, not taking into account weight limits. We swished right past the outer end of the dock, barely slowing as the inevitable drew over us that the boat was going to crash. Jack could not see where the boat left off and the dock started. I was told he once made a dead stop on the freeway during rush to put up the convertible top on his car, now I believed it.

The boat crashed into the sidewalk by the dock, quickly sinking. We scrambled to get out of the boat and into the water, where we could hold on to the dock pillars and climb the ladder up the side. We crawled out one at a time and I stood in my wet suit (not the surfing kind) watching the bubbles emerge to the surface, popping gaily back to the atmosphere, everybody laughing their wet asses off. We found our way back to his car and got in soaking wet. I politely thanked him for the lunch and the ride and he answered, "You are welcome."

As it turned out, he had ripped off a partner he had in the past from New York. People in the agency seemed to know that the partner (and the law) was looking for him. Long after I left this agency, I got a call from a fellow who said he owed Jack some money and was trying to find him.

"Sure," I thought.

So I told the guy where Jack lived and he thanked me. Jack and his company disappeared soon after that.

Jack was clearly crazy. He thought that to be successfully dishonest you had to be smart. Many people believe this. I hope this writing demonstrates the problem with such thought in business. There is a quality of life a business should provide as a whole both internal and external. If the wrong person heads it, or it has no real purpose or accomplishment in it, then there is no quality to be had.

These people are all around us, lurking to take us whenever possible. If it seems too good to be true, it probably is. From a consumer standpoint, it is a huge red flag if the person just does not seem to have the space between their ears adjusted properly. Even worse are those people who appear too nice or too eager to represent your best interest. If they are standing on piles of money, in a flashy office, with a new Mercedes, beware. Honest people often mistake these indices as success. Nice people are all too often the people that lie and steal your money from you. That was Jack.

But I do not mean to single him out, as you will see.

What most people, consumers, clients and those who depend on the honesty of business, seldom see is the inner workings of these businesses. The cashier, the receptionist, the offices and those at the periphery of the business organization seldom know what is really going on by the top insiders and actually help give that particular organization a façade of acceptability, a reason to believe it is honest and credible no matter what or who is really going on. The receptionist may have a smile in her voice but that has nothing to do with what lurks within.

People seldom realize that business is run by humans and humans are mostly flawed. What one has to watch out for is just how flawed some of these people are no matter the appearance. Personality traits – kind, gruff, sweet, amiable, and excitable and the like - have nothing to do with the trustworthiness of the person you willingly pay for service or product.

More than once, it occurred to me that sometimes the person at the top could become the one for the rest in the company to carry. When the owner becomes the obstacle, there is no option to fire or replace them. This can happen if the top person is incompetent but has a lot of capital to work with, or has employees who will pick up their slack.

There was a tacit agreement among the employees of the company to be the ones to keep our organization buoyant long enough for us to survive. Buoyant until a new opportunity would come along. When the CEO of a large company becomes the obstacle, it will become apparent and he will be replaced, even if it takes years. This is why deals for "golden parachutes" are never a good idea. If I had to draw from particular facets of knowledge based on the Jack experience, it would include the fact that business, like all of human life, is dynamic. There is ebb and flow reflected by Jack's statement in one of his more lucid moments, "you can lose an account in the blink of an eye." This is especially true in the life of an agency based on advertising or public relations but is not always understood by other types of companies where it is just as true. Nothing is stagnant, be it economic or personal. The customer is always giving and taking away. Customers are always buying then leaving. A business is like the flow of a river, the manager standing or moving ahead. The moment a business stops moving ahead the river passes it by. This is the reason growth is mandatory for a company's survival. As opposed to thinking that growth is only necessary for competitive reasons.

Chapter Three

I was out to find a new opportunity in Public Relations and I found it in the local city magazine. The "Top Fifty" people most likely to succeed were reviewed in this rag as a yearly article. The magazine pushed the people they thought would stand tall including the bios and pictures of these people as among the lowly average American in town. Most of them I had never heard of so I am certain they were either pals of people in the magazine or people doing business with the magazine. They were meant as favors to those in it as most of these things are.

There was this one very strange looking person in Top 50 pictures, considered the head of an "up and coming" PR agency. He was a new founder of a PR agency and apparently doing well. That sounded like an opportunity to me, hitching on to a comer of an agency so that I could take credit for its progress. It was a perfect format for self-promotion and glory claiming.

He had started his new agency having been a journalist for the once powerful paper in town. He was an investigative reporter who had reported a huge financial fraud in the city worth many billions involving at least two banks and a city hero. People went to jail, including the city hero, and this guy was nominated for the Pulitzer Prize for his reporting.

In looking back at my experience with him, I think he was a deer in the headlights caught in the public relations and marketing communications industry, foreign to journalism, or, in my opinion it should be foreign to journalism. He clearly had an ego the size of Mount Everest yet finding himself in a land he knew nothing about. He was like a doctor caught in the world of finance, not having a clue but sure yhat his brains would bail him out in the end. Because of his journalistic notoriety, people in high places who were also good friends with the people he had put in jail respected and feared him. He and his new PR agency accompanied big developers to meetings with government boards and red-tape ensconced bureaucracies, pleading their cases to rape and pillage the land. Throughout the business community, he was known as the fellow who had brought down one of the largest, wealthiest and most powerful fellows bringing a certain unearned degree of fear. What that did for him as a PR professional remains uncertain but it may have come in handy for connections.

I gave him a call and pitched the wonders of my talents and the sheer mental prowess of my strategic thinking in the ways of marketing and PR. He gave me some bogus test, which was supposed to measure my intelligence and level of organization. I thought it was a creative test but it turns out I was wrong. It was supposed to discover if I was organized or not, rather than rating my creativity. My level of organization was based on the most creative and artistic painting I could think of.

As it turned out, he was a 10 on the 10-point organization scale. He was looking for people just like himself - never a good idea for a business startup. A smart founder should identify and attract a diverse group of employees, like the founder of the racquetball startup did.

I failed the organized part of the test miserably, through my penchant for abstract art. Part of the test did not show me as very organized. However, I rated so high in intelligence that the owner of the up and coming PR agency hired me as an account executive. That title gave me some of my mojo back.

The morning came when I was to report to my new job for the man that the magazine described as "the coolest dude in Public Relations." I slugged down my cup of legal speed and chewed on what tasted like an old shoe for breakfast that morning. It was time to meet my new company, where my expectations were for all things fun, good and true. I got into my car and started the trek to the freeway toward downtown among the tall buildings and up to the 17th floor in a new building where my office overlooking the bay, where a fat salary awaited me, along with all the official and unofficial benefits that would be mine to behold.

I should have noticed it right away as I arrived to the reception area. The smell of estrogen was in the air knocking me over the second I walked into the place. It was no wonder the "orientation" I was shown was nothing more than six hours of sexual harassment training. There were 38 women in this place and I was one of three men. The founder of this PR agency was always in a "meeting" with any female that casually walked into his office. We had to schedule days in advance to discuss a million dollar issue. Lord help you if you did not show up with an agenda in hand. A meeting was never to go over an hour and one must never stray from the meeting agenda. Pretty good rule I think but it should have applied to everyone.

He played personal ogre to us males with his best micromanaging style. He was like a walking horror machine ambling down the hall into your office without notice. He was a direct channel to the monster that scared the bejesus out of you as a child watching your first scary movie. It became painfully evident he kept the women around for satisfaction of his little boy psyche, seeking approval from the female species who manipulated him like meat in a sausage factory. He kept the men around as his personal whipping boys to brow beat, creating such a negative environment it bordered on criminal.

The company was in a posh, new building with snazzy offices high over downtown overlooking the bay. It was beautiful and miserable all in one sick package. Clients were taken to a bright, new reception area then to a meeting place with expensive modern furniture, great art and plush carpet. The finest of rare wood and an exquisite wine collection was available in there, all suggesting a quality-driven, successful business. Nothing could have been further from reality.

The founder of the company had a system of communication where each person had his own mailbox slot in the mailroom where everyone left notes for each other. Messages were hand-written and left in your mailbox. Messages where then collected by the box owner, answered in pen, and returned to the other guy's mailbox. There was no talking allowed, it was considered a waste of time, better spent working. You could have heard a pin drop in that company. The owner's favorite trick was to leave you some task or project in your box that you could not make hide nor tail of, then explode if you dare ask him for clarification. His notes were hand written with illegible scribble asking things like "stick four sheep under the water for a couple weeks then get back with sand box and fritters." I swear that is what it said.

One note he left me was explicit that I "not do what other sham cars equate in the mars ban from this moment to do square."

I saved that note. I still have it somewhere. I typed a note back to him asking him how I should interpret this and if there might be some kind of deadline to it. The next morning he threw my office door open stomping to my desk red-faced, yelling at me for having triple spaced the note. A format I preferred in notes for spatial reasons. Everyone in the company could hear as he yelled that no one else would do anything like this, and then slammed the note down on my desk in front of me. I sat stunned in disbelief as he turned and stomped back out. I was humiliated.

Gawd almighty, I thought. This little bastard is nuts. Nevertheless, I was able to bring many big, well-paying clients to this agency. As the lack of appreciation for having done this set in, I committed to making some kind of move to relieve this problem person so prevalent in my life. Was it me or those that employed me? I asked myself. Am I nuts or are they? I had to ask what the differencewas between where it all seemed so sane and smooth back at the startup company.

Talk about faulty employment practice! He hired friends and family of his biggest and most important clients thinking it good for client relations. One person was a graphics designer, who was somehow connected to a major player in the law community and a major client. I brought in a client who was a very large developer who had a very specific idea as to what an advertisement should look like, never mind he hired us to come up with a concept based on solid marketing. When a client insists on doing something like that, you try to give your best guidance but know when to back off. I brought his idea to the graphic designer in question and she refused to produce it! Her relation to the other big client gave her power and she knew it. She also had the advantage of being a female in the company and the ear of the boss. I was doomed. I was stuck between a rock and a hard place.

In hindsight, I should have "scheduled" a meeting with an agenda to include the graphic designer and the boss and explain what was at stake if the graphic designer flew in the face of our client explaining we would lose the client. Instead, knowing what her position was, I took her idea to the client-developer and did my best to convince him of its value. He was enraged. He resigned as a client and it was my entire fault, of course. An employee should be hired on merit, never for some connection like this. The other lesson learned is that of communication. Let the boss know where the rock and hard place are, and then let the chips fall where they may.

I must admit that later I made the classic mistake of talking about the old boss, Jack, and his crazy antics to the new boss. You need an especially stable, secure person as a boss to do this. It brings out the fear that they might be exactly like the boss you are talking about, or worse, talk about what a terrible boss they are in the same way. It could be code for what they are in the eye of their employees.

He was short, out of his element, a hero of the past and knew little of what he had to do outside of write stories for his clients and sell these stories to editors, which he could do as he was from that world. He knew little about marketing communications. He had spent much time attempting to overcome this. Another problem he had was with brushing shoulders with major clients who towered over him financially and in accomplishment.

Real estate developers were prevalent at this time, with a real estate boom and downtown expansion. I could always get these people to our agency because of the founders' background in journalism and my understanding of the crazed outlook of the developer-visionary. He had a longing to be as visionary and as wild as these entrepreneurs were. The problem was he just did not possess such a bone in all his body. Big time developers are not like your average person. They are willing to drag bankers through the mud and engineers to the gates of hell and contractors to the brink of bankruptcy to fulfill their dream of huge monuments to tribute themselves and great wealth. Building fancy structures and sprawling, luxurious hotels does not take as much intelligence as it does sheer guts and willingness to tough it out and bully your way through government red tape, spending gargantuan amounts on the best lawyers. It takes motivation to get it all through, buying the land without the original landowner being aware of why the land is wanted. These were the people he wanted to be but was not.

I stood at my office window looking out over the bay, a huge oil tanker moored in the center looking like a toy from where I was. It looked like it was taking up a good portion of the bay slowly swaying from side to side from the incoming tide. It would take maybe an hour for it to move in a 45-degree angle and back from where it was moored. It was a Zen thing that seemed to help keep me sane, and then one day the tanker was gone.

It was a great view out of that office but somehow that seemed little consolation in the face of a mad man bent on sticking my brain in a meat grinder, doing his damndest to send me to the sanitarium. The view out my office sometimes served as sort of a window of instant peace where I could escape for a moment and I was doing just that when it hit me like the sharp edges of a broken rum bottle. Why was I bringing in money for this person when I could be bringing in money at my own establishment? By now, I had the expertise, the connections and talent to pull it off on my own. All it would take was guts.

I was instantly committed and I had to act fast. At the end of the next day, I packed all my contact records in a small box, walked down the hall into the founder's office and flipped my key onto his desk saying, "It's me and four sheep over the wall, Sir. I am out of here." He gave me a look of sadness, saying nothing, which I did not understand. He had been treating me like so much dog crap stuck to his shoe and he was sad to see me go?

He always introduced me to clients as his "marketing guru" yet would say things in front of them to put me down in the office. I soon understood he hired me because he thought the person doing the hiring was the superior human.

The agency I worked for in the high beautiful building with the bay view seemed solid enough on the outside. Years later, he hired several people from successful companies attempting to save his company. No one could and it finally went out of business. No matter whom he brought in to do what, he always won out because he was the owner and the boss. It never stood a chance. He later opened a partnership agency and of course, that was short lived. He now has his own semblance of an agency, tries to validate himself through memberships in all things PR. He wrote a book on his theory of PR, not really an intelligent read. It is as though people in business who have this intractable view of the world believe the world is actually, as they think it should be, not the way it is.

After that job, I took a short gig as a stopgap at an advertising agency. It was founded by a very nice looking woman with the disposition of a Pit Bull hyped on a combination of LSD and elephant tranquilizer. She called me at home to offer me a job. She heard I was good at getting clients so I thought, why not?

She always wore a sneer on that beautiful face and seemed ready to explode at any time, yet she faded into the smiling beauty upon meetings with clients. There were about 30 people in this agency and it became obvious there was one artist whose work was supporting the entire company. Clients and consumers loved his work, and he won awards in New York competitions. The employees, including myself, were mostly bored and quite aware we were being supported by this one guy, and like most bored people in this situation did little more than gossip and bitch about each other to anyone who would listen.

It is interesting how each company has its own persona, its own culture and the persona of each company affects you greatly as its employee no matter how much you try to distance yourself from it all. It is first a social event and second a business.

At my startup racquetball company the money rolled in, everyone was new, we loved each other, and all knew that there was a road ahead that just seemed to get brighter and brighter. Customers raved about our products and the sport of Racquetball and the world seemed to support us. It was beautiful.

When a company is based on baloney, negativity and bogusness, not all is well even if profitable. These businesses are hardly ever long term. I am not sure I can define what the "baloney" is. It may be that the company does not have a real view of what it is about, such as something bigger than making money, having a boss who is not professional, , like the company is not real in its talent and its performance, it feels like a dead end, a black wall. A company based on baloney is the prophet of its own doom, everyone involved understands that on some level and it permeates the organization. A stench roams through the halls and gets into every crevice and pore in the place and your body and your brain. Even if the company is making money and you are getting a check each month there is a black sulfuric fog that seems to make its way into your ears, your heart, your guts and your brain. It makes you wish you had never been born or makes you feel like you should dunk your head in a bucket of water for 10 minutes. It is fear and loathing in business.

Chapter Four

The Fine and the not-so-fine line of Ethics

One of my more interesting clients was a financial company that provided loans to construction companies when they ran out of money during a building project. There is nothing more annoying than building the walls and the floors of a commercial endeavor, such as a recreation complex or luxury apartments, and not having enough money to build the roof. This is usually due to cost overruns, the great bugaboo of the construction industry, and banks. If one runs out of money while building a multimillion-dollar project, it makes sense to borrow enough to finish the damn thing so you can sell it at a profit. You must (emphasis on "must") finish the project or burn it to the ground for the insurance money. However, the latter carries a certain risk factor such as jail time.

When a land developer borrows millions, at a high rate of interest to the company borrowed from, the loaner company makes good money. So how does a privately owned company get its capital to loan? It sends out letters to seniors looking for an income stream to live on from their investments. Their money is then combined in a big pot (corporate account) with other investor's money to loan to needy contractors. The financial company making the loans handles the administration and takes a cut. The go-between loan company makes money as long as there is a lot of building going on.

The president of this financial company contacted my company. I will call this company Construction Capital to keep me from being sued over writing this book... The president was aware that we had recently ranked within the top ten agencies in the city, and his law firm was a client of ours. We will call the President of this company "Chuck."

We immediately set out developing and pitching stories about Chuck's loaning big developers huge amounts of cash known as "bridge money" hence, enabling them to finish the project.

We found ourselves hiring more people from all the business we were getting. The stories about this company were part of the reason we were getting new business in the world of real estate. Golf course projects, huge recreational complexes, tall buildings, luxury residential developments and the like became the common denominator of our work.

Our client pitched potential investor's with a presentation illustrating how they would be getting a check in the mail each month for 10 percent or more on their investment. Sounds good to anybody's ears. Our client had quite a pile of investment money and during the real estate boom he was able to loan money to needy, high-end real estate developments.

When I first took on this financial client, I thought its culture was unique. The second in command, a woman named Pat, was mostly an informal, low-key person who would work alongside the company president then answer the office phones like a receptionist. Pat seemed unhappy but a good person, as was Chuck. Pat was not someone you should cross, you just knew that.

Chuck was a second or third generation immigrant of Mexico and doing quite well for a soft spoken, low-key kind of good-hearted person.

There seemed an anomaly here because a legitimate company has someone running it that is well educated and knows intimate details about finance, taxes and the law. Chuck had no such knowledge or education, just a license to sell real estate. Even his pitch seemed somewhat naïve. At first, I did not understand what Pat was to him as he often referred to her as his partner. However, what the hell, I thought, he does millions in business and always pays my invoice each month. All the articles and press releases I generated, placing in respected local and regional media were building his legitimacy around town.

I soon became his sounding board and trusted comrade in business, yet I was bothered by his lack of knowledge and prowess normally required by a man in his position. Believe me I had seen them all by now. Chuck at Construction Capital took me into his inner circle of trusted allies, which included his father. By some odd warp of the universe, Chuck's father had rented an office one floor underneath my own. His father rather appeared out of nowhere under me and in Chuck's life.

His father's name was Jose, and he was the other side of Chuck. Jose was loud, uneducated, uncultured, obnoxious, short and arrogant. He would stomp around in his steel tipped, snakeskin cowboy boots. Jose had started a business in that downstairs office lending money to people behind in their mortgage payments to help them keep their house. Although I never figured out where his initial capital came from, his business was easy enough to understand. California law states that if you loan money to someone using their property as collateral, and there is signed documentation stating this, you may take their property as soon as they miss a payment, without any court involvement. This was Jose's business, collecting other's properties and often selling the ill-gotten property to his son at low cost. The more I got to know him, the meaner he seemed to be. He was, however, a role model for Chuck and his siblings.

When a recession in real estate comes along, it alters the real estate development landscape altogether. When it hit this time, all building stopped dead in its tracks.

One local, privately held loan company (similar to Construction Capital) was rumored to be its own Ponzi scheme. Before an investment company is deemed a Ponzi scheme, it always looks great to investors.

A Ponzi scheme is a fraudulent investment operation that pays returns to its investors from their own money, or the money paid by subsequent investors, rather than from profit earned by the individual or organization running the operation. The Ponzi scheme usually entices new investors by offering higher returns than other investments. Payments are in the form of short-term returns that are either abnormally high or unusually consistent. Perpetuation of the high returns requires an ever-increasing flow of money from new investors to keep the scheme going.

One high profile, local Ponzi scheme was run from offices in an upscale part of town. Visitors were taken past the Rosewood desks by flashy, well-dressed employees convincing visitors that this was a company doing well. However, the money feeding the company posed as investment was being used to pay off previous clients. Some of it was used to buy the founder yachts, mansions, expensive cars and big vacations. It would be nice to think that the scammers in a Ponzi scheme are only celebrating until the day they go to the pokey. However, it is the opinion of some attorneys who have been involved in some of these schemes that many Ponzi schemes may never be caught. Back to our story.

When the freeze in real estate came, other local construction-based, financial companies shut down or became Ponzi schemes. Chuck hired one of my other clients. Curiously, he hired my client who was a separate law firm asking about the legality of issuing stock without the SEC being involved. When the firm gave Chuck their report, he asked me to interpret it. I was a bit disconcerted that he would ask me to do this rather than the firm that generated that report. I do have a legal background but only as a student of law, not a practicing attorney. Nevertheless, I read it and reported to him that if he kept his stock inside the State, not interstate, he would not have the SEC to worry about. I thought he was doing this to raise more capital and stay away from the gaze of the SEC. I guess he did not realize the SEC was turning its head away from the goings on of graft overall at that time. I was puzzled, for he seemed to be frantically looking for ways to expand. Like most businesses in a recession, he did not realize it was not just his problem but the problem of the economy at large.

Construction Capital was hiring many new people and throwing promotional events for clients as though all was well. There were a lot of vacations and travel scheduled, even though most other companies like this one were either bankrupt or embezzling client funds. My client seemed to be expanding, starting new profitable ventures in an attempt to diversify.

Chuck bought a small lending company with a new handpicked staff to manage it, then asked me to go snoop and interview these managers. I was not at all impressed with any of it and told him so. Like many other companies suffering from the recession, so was this company. No matter where Chuck turned, the recession was always there messing things up.

A few of the competitors were soon tried and sent to jail for absconding investor monies. What troubled me about my client was a lack of announcements about new deals with anyone. Business was dry as a bone and there were many bones around town. It was a hard down recession and this company and its founder in particular, appeared to be flying high, at least from the outside.

As the recession worsened, Chuck spent more time and money hiring new "experts" in their field and throwing promotional events. Chuck must have thought he would have to do something radical and creative in that atmosphere to make money, lest he himself end up in the pokey. It had to have dawned on him that all the spending and fun would end on what was slowly becoming a Ponzi scheme. It was like the famous frog experiment where the frog, being cold blooded, is placed in cool water then the water is heated up so slowly that at some point it becomes too hot for the frog to survive without the frog even realizing it. This was the case with Construction Capital. When the line was crossed from legitimate business to Ponzi scheme, it is hard to notice from the outside. From the inside, the day that investor money is used to pay back investors is the day it becomes Ponzi.

The North American Free Trade Agreement (NAFTA) was developed about this time to take advantage of Mexico's plentiful labor, the U.S.'s technology and Canada's raw materials. Together they would form a united economic powerhouse. Chuck was certain he could take advantage of this buying land in a desert town in South California where his father was well known. This town happened to be one of few entry routes for commercial prospects from Mexico into/through the U.S. thus provoking economic activity in the desert town.

Chuck and his inside group, along with me, began chartering planes back and forth over the mountains of Southern California to meet with community powers in this town. Jose did seem to have influence there from prior real estate dealings or whatever. It was quite an experience taking these flights to this small town. We flew over the mountains barely clearing the tree branches and when we came back, it was nighttime and foggy over those mountains. Somehow, I felt that this was symbolic of what we were doing there. We were just clearing the hurdle, testing what was safe and what could be a very bad thing.

Why did I think we were doing bad things? Chuck was taking suitcases full of cash to this town, returning with empty suitcases. We were delivering cash to people and taking cash from people. During one city council meeting, I came to understood why. Chuck was trying to get a residential development permit from the city to develop a huge area of houses and warehouses to take advantage of the incoming commerce when the NAFTA agreement kicked in. It made sense; truckers from Mexico would be bringing products made by cheap labor from the maquiladoras. That would spawn new business and more population in the town. Lots of people got up in front of that meeting to speak their piece about how this would ruin the town and how it would be an environmental disaster and cut into private property and that many families would have to leave with no place to go.

None of that mattered to anyone on the council. The city leaders pretended to be listening, yawning from time to time, minds already made up by the greasing of the palm I would think. I wondered if this was an unusual event or if it is just the way such matters are done. It all seemed so easy, casual, and so sleight of hand at the same time.

Chuck's father was seemingly always at these meetings in the

51

background and I could not help but notice how people, especially those in high city positions seemed intimidated by him. His attitude was one my father used to call a "Runt Complex," indicating he suffered from being too short to be confident. Jose was well under six feet and compensated with his high-heeled snakeskin boots that matched his awkward, cowboy toughness. His business back in the city was done by intimidating the poor and uneducated slipping their property away from them in the night. He could not have dealt a fair hand in the world of the professional and the honorable. He thought himself smart for outsmarting the desperate out of their money and property.

The night that the development was approved, the entire group of us had meetings with real estate agents in the courthouse like vultures waiting to swoop in on the booty. After the last of these meetings, Jose suggested we all go to a nice Japanese restaurant and have a late dinner before Chuck, Pat and I boarded the plane back to Los Angeles. We all loaded into his car and traveled a few blocks on a hard packed dirt road to a restaurant that was clearly closed. Jose parked right in front of it and since it was closed, I saw no point in getting out, yet everyone else did. Jose walked to the front and stood looking into the unlit restaurant wrapping his knuckles on the glass door as if someone was inside to hear it.

Several long moments went by while Jose kept wrapping on the door. A dim light went on inside and an old Asian couple appeared in back. I was astounded Jose would do this to a pair of elderly, sleeping people who seemed to be living in the back of their business.

"Open up!" Jose yelled at them through the glass.

The old man came forward with his set of keys, recognizing Jose, and let us all into the restaurant. To this day, I wonder what kind of arrangement they had with Jose, or what they owed him.

We all filed in and sat around a large common table. A conversation began, seemingly for my sake, by Jose.

"So did you get your boat back from your pal?" Jose asked Chuck.

"Not yet, but he will bring it back soon," Chuck replied calmly.

"What a wimp-ass, you can't even tell that jerk to bring your boat back now or you will kick him in the ass," Jose said.

Chuck was embarrassed and intimidated by his father and just looked on as though he had not said it, trying to maintain a professional posture.

There were issues about what a man is and what a man does between Chuck and Jose. Pat sat passively as though this was an ongoing scenario. Things were starting to add up in my head. Here was Chuck, doing big deals at a time when no other loaners were, without loaning a dime in months. Yet here he was setting all up all this activity with the help of his father. Something was coming down that smelled bogus.

We ordered dinner from the beer stained menus the old woman had given us. She was small and frail and could not speak

English well, but tried. Pat sat there with the same stoic look she always seemed to have. Never happy about anything yet committed to Chuck and the work in the company and me wondering why he always called her his partner.

She had two shots of Bourbon and the rest of us had a beer. As Chuck and Jose were conversing about how the development project would go, Pat leaned over toward me and quietly told me she wanted to talk to me outside. She stood and asked me if I would like to see some of the town before we left and I agreed. We excused ourselves and strolled out to the street. It was dark and no one was around. It was late and I knew she pulled me out of the restaurant to tell me something. She started talking as if on cue, as if she wanted to tell me her story very much.

"Chuck is my half-brother," she explained. "Chuck's mother is my mother."

"So is Jose your step father?" I asked.

"Not exactly," she said. "Jose and a partner of his had a construction company in these parts. My mother was having an affair with his partner."

She stopped for a moment, gathering courage, as curiosity was rolling through my head.

"Jose came home early one day and found his partner in bed with his wife – my mother. Jose had a pistol he kept in the bed stand and he was drunk and he pulled out the gun and shot his partner dead in bed with my mother."

She stood with the dim street lamp behind her keeping her

face in a shadow. I could not see her expression but the glint coming from her eyes was giving me a strong hint as to what her next statement might be.

"My father was the man Jose killed that night." She said this almost as if it was no big deal. "My mother was pregnant by the man she was having an affair with and that was Jose's partner – my father."

I stood looking at her, dumbfounded... I could not find any appropriate words. A few seconds of silence passed, broken only by the sounds of cars in the distance passing on the hard dirt road. Chuck's relationship to Pat became suddenly as clear to me as the glass door in the restaurant. Jose and Chuck owed her something and she felt like a child who had been dumped accidently on the universe, the product of craziness and a gun. I felt very sorry for her and her built- in sadness about who she was. How was I going to walk back into that restaurant acting as if nothing had happened? However, no, she had to go on and tell me more.

"Jose was apprehended and tried for second degree murder. He was found guilty by a jury and sentenced to 15 years in the penitentiary. He learned a lot of bad things while he was in there," she said. "He learned to be merciless and evil. He taunts Chuck all the time about how soft he is. He gets Chuck the money from older people in this town and shows Chuck how to extract it from them. Chuck is not really like him yet he wants to live up to his expectations and he never will."

I now understood this odd dynamic duo between father and son. Son is a nice person but not tough enough to satisfy dad. Son feels he is a disappointment to his murderous father. Father rides son on being too soft on the world. Son must do something evil to satisfy father.

Chuck always seemed a professional person and used it as a wall between himself and other people. You always walked away from a conversation with him wondering who he was.

Pat and I walked back to the restaurant. As we walked in, Jose was in some kind of tirade. He was telling Chuck about how this was a "dog eats dog" world and he had to do what he did to be successful.

Jose was one of those people who thought that you had to be crooked or immoral to make money. I am not sure if he really believed this or if he just enjoyed it. His business of loaning money to mortgage holders, then yanking the property out from under them the day after a missed payment, was legal but certainly immoral. In addition, he was a proud little man because of it.

He was giving Chuck a strategy. Now that the city council had been paid off for approving the "development" in town moves had to be made. Corporate Construction had to look like it was doing well in spite of the downturn in real estate and commercial development. Casual trips were made to faraway countries where banks were not held accountable by U.S. authority for deposits.

Chuck started hiring more and more people for the once five-person company. He had more "events" for his investors showing them a good time and how well the company was doing at the same time. His business moved into a new and fancy high-rise building with huge offices and high-end furnishings. Yet there had been no announcements of any kind of new business and loans for commercial development. I knew something was up and I felt Jose was behind this whole thing somehow, egging Chuck on.

Pat must have known what was happening but she just trudged on as if all was well. She did begin to make personal changes. She worked out each day and wore clothing other than baggy pantsuits. She was becoming a beautiful sexy woman and seemingly happier. The story she told me must have been a load off her shoulders. She said she had never told anyone else.

The property in the desert Chuck had bought just sat there. No development was taking place and I could not help but wonder what the next move would be.

We started to make trips more frequently to our desert town again, visiting various real estate agents from Mexico. We met these agents in local bars with what seemed to me rather seedy people. I was never sure why we were making the trips and why I was required to go along. I could only surmise that I gave Chuck some kind of legitimacy as his PR person and advisor, maybe providing something of a professional air. He never told me exactly what was going on. I did not ask.

We always went and returned over the mountaintops with those suitcases. On one of those trips, our pilot was a bit tipsy. I assumed he was sober enough to fly or he would not have gotten behind the wheel…but I was wrong.

We were over the top of the mountains on a return trip late at night; I could just make out the trees below in the moonlight, thinking we were much too close to those trees. If we came across taller trees, we were going to be in for it. I heard a slight brushing sound underneath the floor of the plane getting louder and louder. Way too damn loud for comfort. Just to be sure, all was under control in the cockpit I stood up from my seat and looked toward the front windshield past the pilot. I could see the shapes of the other passengers all comfortable and asleep in my periphery. The brushing sound was getting more audible. As I peered out the front, I could see the silhouette of a tall tree in the moonlight we were heading directly toward. Two very fast steps took me next to the sleeping pilot, to pull back on the steering. The scraping branches of tree branches woke the pilot and everyone else up. Sweat was running down my forehead. I could barely feel myself breathing, as we seemed to have averted the disaster of running headlong into a mountain pine.

"God damn it to shit!" I heard the words come out of my mouth. "What are you doing sleeping while you are flying this clap trap?" I yelled at the pilot.

He just looked up at me with a dazed look and shrugged slowly, taking back the wheel. I went back to my seat, all eyes were upon me.

"Your pilot fell asleep Chuck and almost ran us into a tree!" I yelled to him over the propeller noise. "I think you should look somewhere outside Alcoholics Anonymous for your next driver over these god damn mountains next time."

He nodded his head in agreement and quickly fell back to sleep, taking just a moment to check the suitcase full of cash under his seat.

Meanwhile, a local columnist was starting to take note of all the business failures in real estate around town. There had been a boom in southern California during that particular decade and people from the cold north were escaping to the warmer climate. "Snow birds" we called them in the real estate industry.

Along with the boom came the invasion of big businesses from out of state seeking to make a fortune from the local developing economy. Many of these businesses understood the need for public relations and publicity, touting their doings and good names as plastered in key media. It made all the difference to a new firm in town and the larger professional firms used it. My firm was the best agency for professionals in town at this stage and they knew it. My clients included architectural firms, engineering firms, law firms, large accounting, construction, developers and financial firms. I felt the company diversified but at the end of the real estate boom, the big out-of-town professional firms pulled up stakes and left along with the real estate business.

Nevertheless, a business needs to move ahead and get as much business as possible lest the river of commerce carry it backwards into oblivion. I needed to keep business wherever I could find it and Chuck's loan business was one of my few loyal clients. He seemed to relish my advice and experience.

By now, I was in the top of the Heavy Hitters list in town, the "Top 10 firms in town, and in the Who's Who of the World in marketing communications and finance. I had what competitors wanted if only they knew how to get it. It is important to attain these accolades you can share with clients. This is the privilege of professional know how.

The local columnist I mentioned fancied himself as the whistleblower of all things evil in business. As commercial construction loan companies started to go under, a couple became Ponzi schemes. I could understand how the successful owner of a company who was enjoying the life of luxury might milk the good times even after they had passed. The only way to do that was to keep on delving into investor's money until it was gone, then admit the wrongdoing and go to prison.

I was asking myself about Chuck's company for some time. I was puzzled by his hiring spree and against all odds growth, until I went to that restaurant in the desert with his father and half-sister. I somehow knew what was going on after that. In addition, I knew that the day would come when he would stand before a judge and explain where all of the investor's money had gone.

Chuck would stand there and say, "The money is all gone, your honor, I spent it all to try to save my company."

To me it looked as though he had taken trips to safe havens in foreign countries in order to save the money. Somehow, I could not fathom him getting in front of the judge saying, "Well it's a good thing I have a few million in Jamaica, the Canary Islands, the Bahamas, and China your Honor."

At some point, the money was all gone from the company. I had trouble running down my monthly retainer check. The last of those checks bounced so I took a personal trip to the company finding the doors closed and locks across the doors. The local columnist had gotten wind and would not let up. He started calling me for information and I never returned a call. Somehow, he got the information anyway. The columnist was able to describe very specific scenes where I was alone with Chuck and his father. Jose had to have been feeding the columnist information about Chuck and the company. He was actually helping make his son a bad boy like himself, to make himself proud of his son. I just could not believe it but it had to be true.

It was even worse than that. Chuck was proud of his notoriety, his transformation as a white collar criminal who stole his investor's money to "save his company" as it were. He was becoming the son his father would be proud of.

I attended parts of his trial and there was evidence he was selling his acquired land for cash to Mexican moneymen which must have been the cash we were bringing home over the mountains in suitcases. Chuck was given a four-year sentence for 22 counts and is now free living in the south of France.

Chapter Five

Legal Ethics

A deep pockets law client: wrong time, wrong place.

I mentioned a famous Ponzi scheme that took place in town by a fellow posing as a "currency trader." He claimed to be raking in money with the promise of a 40 percent return on investment. His top floor offices sat in a posh building in the high-end district, overlooking a beautiful Pacific cove. To get a picture of the sheer size of this scheme, there was a $200M international arbitrage involved during a 9-year period and in the 1980s, this was a considerable sum in those days. At that time, it was the largest Ponzi scheme in history. He suffered a stroke in prison and died while serving a 20-year sentence. Since then there have been larger such schemes, the latest being the Bernie Madoff case.

The fellow heading this 1980 Ponzi was an egg headed introvert void of any charisma or charm whatsoever. We ran into each other from time to time at various local events, his connections mostly tied to his girlfriend, the mayor of a well-to-do coastal community in southern California. She had many parties for the wealthy people she knew and her influence was sought after by a wide network of them. She was involved in all the black-tie gala events, rubbing shoulders with those that possessed enough money to fund her charities and her boyfriend. J David sat back and watched as she scooped money from her high powered yet gullible friends to feed into his scheme.

Ethics seldom involves a split-second choice, even though a

court of law assumes that. How can we not think of someone who takes money from others with no intention of delivering a return as evil? However, who among us would refuse a check sliding across a restaurant table for one million dollars? As the owner of a sleek Mercedes AMG, a Rolls Royce, Bentley and a Corvette, attending wonderful parties all over the world, would we really say no to that check? Would luxurious vacations in exotic places, meeting celebrities and attending their parties seem more attractive than shoving that check back to the writer of it? In addition, if this had been going on because your girlfriend or boyfriend had pals frothing at the mouth to give you a part of their fortune just so you could keep up this life style, would you do the right thing and turn it all down? Then go back to a one-room apartment with the hanging light bulb, living on canned pork shoulder? Moreover, what if you had the impression the scheme could go on forever?

Ethics is always a balance between the amount of money involved and how close and real the consequences (like jail) are. If the money is good and the threat of consequences seem unlikely; the more ethics becomes measurable on a sliding scale from "the right thing" on one side showing slight consequence to "the wrong thing" on the side of consequences seen as a real possibility.

J David, our Ponzi scheme fellow recognized here, hired some of the best law firms money can buy. They told him that he was going to be fine; his funds would be secure with the exception of a bank account in Montserrat. Then when it was all starting to

63

unfold, these same attorneys met in London to discuss how to keep him afloat until they received money owed them. What they should have discussed was how to stay off the FBI's radar.

J David's attorney was a member of a well-known law firm, housed in the same building as his own, two floors down. When the case blew open, investors received very little of their money back therefore, as a unit they filed what is known as "deep pockets" style litigation against any legal/professional representation for this scheme.

In the context of a lawsuit, the "deep pocket" is often the target defendant, even when the true (moral) culpability is with another party (J David) because the deep pocket has money to pay a verdict. For example, a lawyer may comment that he or she sued the manufacturer of a product rather than the seller because it is the deep pocket, meaning it has more money than the seller with which to compensate the victim. An assumed linage of responsibility is drawn from deep pocket to the culpable.

Most of the large professional firms who were implicated in their explicit or implicit involvement in the scheme settled with the investors. The largest of these firms settled for $60 million.

The law firm two floors below refused to settle on the personal grounds that they were not part of his wrongdoing. I was involved as a strategic partner with that law firm. The Ponzi investment victims stood firm that my firm had aided and abetted this fellow in running his scheme.

I received a call in my offices from a fellow by the name of

Gary, who was a founding partner of the firm being sued by investors for representing J David.

J David was thought to have been a genius trader of currencies, which was an almost impossible way to make money back then. The upper echelon in town thought him legitimate as he had offices in the most upscale part of town with very nice appointments of class and money, Rosewood furniture, beautiful receptionist and handsome representatives. He drove the finest of cars and lived in the best parts of a multi-million dollar mansion community. How could this be a fraud? He promised huge returns and folks with lots of money believed it because their pals had invested in this scammer's company. When it was discovered that this person was running a Ponzi scheme people panicked causing a classic run of the withdrawal of funds, thus collapsing the company. J David's claim to fame, oddly enough, is that before Allen Stanford, Bernie Madoff and Art Nadel came along; he was America's biggest Ponzi All-Star.

When he went down, so did a number of politicians in town, including the mayor, who was taking illegal funding from J David to run his campaign. The mayor was later convicted on 13 felony counts but later he got off on a technicality. He is now a conservative radio talk show host on a level similar to Rush Limbaugh.

J David was tried, convicted and sent to prison for more than 20 years and has since died. He suffered a stroke while in prison while talking to the same girlfriend who acted as the source of his ill-gotten gains. She ended up serving two years in prison then bounced back by marrying a wealthy person who later died leaving her his money. She then married another wealthy fellow.

Regardless of all the criminal activity and fraud I write about here this chapter is written with love. One of my life long best friends was Gary, the founding partner I mentioned in the law firm sued by investors who was ironically the finest legal mind in the region. He and his law firm were the most outrageously successful firm in town. We had many strategic meetings regarding the dilemma his firm was in because of its involvement in the J David fiasco. We talked of his grandchildren, my children, his time in Korea as a young man, personal philosophies, hopes and dreams and various types of legal machinations. He indicated to me that if this litigation by these investors were successful, he would retire.

Gary litigated antitrust and commercial cases throughout the United States for 30 years with a 93.57 percent trial success rate. He was the senior partner of this largest independent law firm in California.

As a young man, Gary started out working as ranch hand in Colorado for his grandfather. He pursued his professional life as a Sheriff's deputy while finishing law school at night. His first case was spent representing a fellow who started a small kiosk-style business where customers dropped off their exposed film and picked up their finished pictures as a drive through. The Kodak Corporation started copying his style with their own kiosks around town and Gary was hired to sue Kodak for using his client's business trade model/service mark winning $20 million from Kodak.

Upon retirement, Gary moved to a small California town and wrote a few books with his wife about United States history. He was a genuine fellow and a true legal genius with a major humor streak. I will always be grateful for his friendship and camaraderie. He died September 6, 2011 when he was 79 year old.

After hiring me, Gary spent several days with me detailing the entire story of his firm and J David so that I could be more effective in representing his firm to the media. If the firm lost this case, members of his firm could be disbarred and he felt this unjust and wrong.

He told me he was as cognizant as anyone else about the J David scheme and that was not so much. A previous partner in the firm had been J David's personal lawyer but was "no longer with the firm."

Gary asked me the first day we met if I had known about this previous partner and what his relationship was with the J David company. I let him know I did not know anything about the departed partner. He went on to tell me that they had let this partner, who had a background in divorce and domestic law, work with J David upstairs on a daily basis who was bringing in huge revenues for his firm. Apparently, he was riding herd over J David's trades and then destroying records. That partner, who they had to dismiss, was using J David money to pay the mortgage on his fine home overlooking the ocean and was taking out investments at J David with fake names like "Blackstone" based in Montserrat.

Both the largest and most respectable law firm in the country and one of the largest and most respectable accounting firms had indicated all was well with J David, so Gary had let it ride up to this point. Now they were telling him there could be a problem. Later, insiders of these large firms tipped Gary off that J David would not let them see certain overseas accounts in Montserrat, so their audits may not have covered everything.

"That was just what I wanted to hear," Gary told me. "For years all was well and we get some fine revenues from this company, then all hell breaks loose and we are on the butt end of a suit. You can be driving home, content and happy, whistling 'Happy Day' when out of nowhere, like a bolt of lightning hits you, you are zapped by a suit. People who think if they do nothing wrong in their own personal journal that they will not suffer the long arm of the law are treading water until it happens. There was no way I could have seen this thing coming and prevented it."

Rather than go to trial, these largest law and accounting firms settled with bilked investor's for more than $60 million after it was discovered this was a Ponzi scheme they had "audited."

Gary and I held strategic lunch meetings across the street from his building in a well-known, upscale restaurant, reserved by Gary's firm to keep it empty. He did this so we would be alone with no stray ears to hear what was being said.

At one meeting, we had lunch with people who had as much influence as Gary with the restaurant, they were Joan Crock, wife of McDonald's owner Ray Crock and the owner of the local NFL franchise. We had lunch together, our usual strategy meeting turning into a social occasion with these two, which turned out well as I picked up another client from it.

Gary told me that the FBI asked him to J David, he took them straight up to the J David offices on the top floor then left them with J David alone. The FBI agents would later attest to that in the trial.

"For God's sake, would I have left him alone with two FBI agents if I had thought he had committed crimes and my firm representing him?" He said.

He had a point all right.

One morning Gary came into his offices, me waiting, without as much as a "good morning." He immediately launched into a scenario.

"Should the defense attorney for Juan Corona be convicted of murder or be sued in a civil case because he represented a serial killer?" Gary asked in frustration. "There is a client-attorney relationship that has to be sacred to the long arm of the opposition and without that, an attorney cannot do his job which is to give the best possible defense to his client."

During our talk about legal matters, things got a bit sticky. We were looking at client-attorney privilege and subsequent theory as a defense. It worked and yet something was off.

He was applying the client-attorney relationship to the relationship between his firm and J David. If a client tells his attorney every detail of the crime and the details would seem to point to the client being guilty, the attorney has a moral and a professional obligation to defend his or her client in the most profound manner possible. The law demands this client-attorney privilege hold. As an officer of the court, an attorney is obligated to listen to the client's side and keep that information quiet as sacred trust. So an attorney cannot become accountable for not telling anyone, including the court, about the crime. Yet J David had said nothing to Gary about his crimes. So is it legal protocol to accuse or expose your client when you have no knowledge of any wrongdoing? The court did not seem to be sophisticated enough to apply this.

Another angle was the work-product doctrine more inclusive than attorney–client privilege. Unlike the attorney–client privilege, which includes only communications between an attorney and the client, work-product includes materials prepared by persons other than the attorney. The materials may have been prepared by anybody as long as they were prepared with an eye towards the realistic possibility of impending litigation. This includes materials collected for the attorney such as interrogatories, signed statements and other information acquired for the prosecution or defense of a case. However, memoranda, briefs, communications and other writings prepared by counsel for their own use in the client's case (mental impressions, conclusions, opinions, or legal theories) are never discoverable by an opposing party.

What did happen in court was political and was caused by the dynamics of events based on influence, and those involved. These influential investors had been taken by J David and someone had to pay the price. These victims held influence with people of the court and they had been duped right under their noses and made to look like assholes. It was the dynamics of the town.

Even well-educated adults can have a hard time understanding the risks and payoffs associated with financial deals — a fact of which shady operators are all too aware. How many of us know what is actually in our credit card contracts yet how many of us want to admit we were taken by the fine print?

Gary and I discussed how the court might see this as a matter of Agency and it did. Agency refers to a company's employees as legal "agents" acting on behalf of and under the control of the company when dealing with a third party. An agent represents the business by acting as an appendage of the company. If the agent breaks the law while under contract, then the company becomes responsible. As a business owner, if you have an employee who is going to commit a crime, they had best commit it on their own time.

Take Juan Corona for example, who killed twenty people and buried them under his house. Per our constitution, everyone deserves a defense and someone had to defend him. Could the victims' families have sued the defense attorney for his association with their relatives' murderer like a "deep pockets" case? Not by any reasonable or legal grounds.

As one of the best attorneys in town could, Gary had convinced me that he and his firm were being chased for having been in the wrong place at the wrong time and highly influential investors in J David were baying for blood.

Law firms have been using PR to sway the public through the media for years; and is a technique widely understood in the legal industry. Gary was attempting to do the same through my firm and myself. After all, anyone in the public could potentially become part of a jury. Judges and prosecutors are influenced by what is in the "news," even if planted in the media by a good public relations strategist.

Gary said that J David had "all the indices of success" and he never had reason to doubt what was going on. The J David clients received their investment money plus great interest. The partner, or girlfriend of J David was a former mayor of Del Mar and had connections with all of the moneyed factors in town. She was closely connected with the mayor of the city, he was eventually taken down because of it.

In Gary's words, "If every wealthy person in San Diego County trusts the guy, why were we not supposed to? If the mayor of Del Mar and the mayor of San Diego was his pal, why were we supposed to have uncovered some wrong doing he was into." I could not really come up with any counter arguments to his.

As mentioned before, over the course of maybe 10 meetings, Gary proceeded to tell me every detail of his relationship with J David. When he came to the present time in the story, he made the following statement.

"This is an ongoing case and you are now part of it, and now that I have told you everything there is no part of it you can reveal as a material witness because this is a privileged client-attorney relationship and you will let anyone who asks you know that. I cannot reveal what you tell me as well."

I was stunned. I was now in the very center of the whole thing. At that moment, I realized I was a thread in the weave of a huge matter of the law known widely to the public. At first, it was quite humbling. This was the biggest news story of the region garnering large chunks of time on local, regional and national news media. I was on the inside of an ongoing news media event and I had to be very careful what I said and to whom. When I made media contact, I had to know what I was going to say and how I would say it and no more. As the means of contact and information for the firm, I was somewhat overwhelmed at times. Our strategy meetings in the famous restaurant kept things square and straight with the media and me. At times, I felt in awe of what I seemed to be in the middle of, yet I had to pretend to myself this was just another day and another bucket of cash.

As the reality of it set in, the challenge became invigorating and energizing; I realized how it must have felt to be an attorney involved in big and important cases and a media hound. "I suggest we do some research to see just what the legal industry and the public thinks of you." I told him and he agreed.

We performed research but found no surprises. The average person on the street had no clue what or who Gary's firm was and little understanding of why they were being sued. Legal people knew exactly who they were and why they were in hot water and mostly had an attitude resembling the old adage "but for the grace of God go I."

This was Gary's law firm, and being accused of doing such wrong on the side of a person like J David challenged his sense of who he was. He hated the doubt it cast on his integrity.

It so happened that Gary had accepted an elderly investor's case who had major problems with his money and E.F. Hutton, a now defunct brokerage that ran a series of advertisements claiming that "when E.F Hutton talks, people listen" and that was my headline for a story which I posed to an editor as a "press release." The headline read, *When Investors Speak, E.F. Hutton Listens*.

Gary won the case for the elderly investor, winning millions in compensation and punitive awards. His name will remain without mention here but my article, exactly as written, hit the top front page of a major daily newspaper. For some reason the brokerage firm had not listened to Gary's client when he instructed them to buy him quality bonds, then froze his money when he complained. Gary told me that when he checked to see just how many suits like this were filed against E.F. Hutton, he found many. Funny how nothing really changes. Here we are years later and big well known firms are found guilty of idiotic tomfoolery on a consistent basis. People continue to trust them though and still get hurt.

Why is consumer financial protection necessary? Because fraud and abuse happen each day on a legal and a not-so-legal basis. Even educated and informed consumers cannot well take care of themselves. Not all consumers are educated and informed. Our culture worships material wealth over friendship, happiness, kindness, paying any price or risking to achieve wealth. It is a vision of dystopia, where people are battling one another, in congress and on the streets and banks of our country. That is the sad reason that we need government help to protect us from ourselves rather than do the bidding of the influential and the wealthy. People should watch the classic American musical <u>The Music Man</u> again. The whole town is fooled by a charismatic, fun-loving charlatan. Just like it happens way to much America.

As a matter of strategy, the Mr. "investor" versus E.F. Hutton case looked as though Gary had helped an elderly investor. All the while, his firm had a suit filed against it by elderly J David investors. We had hoped the irony would dawn on the public. I milked this story all the way to 60 Minutes, where it was accepted and recorded, but never aired. Local media took my updates on the Hutton story and used the information in their news items, keeping the heroics of my client above the fray of what was going on underneath.

My firm and writers pushed the envelope on this client, as we knew there was an injustice going on. Law firms already have a certain bias against them by the public. Even when they do the right thing, they are assumed wrong and evil. There are honest lawyers and I have known and worked with many. Gary and his firm were just in the wrong place at the wrong time. When they represented the most notorious and largest Ponzi schemer of the time it was no fault of their own. It did not help that their partner was a financial legal novice, desperate and in over his head with a life style he could not support, making an unethical decision.

The legal premise of "Agency" won when it came down to the political nature of the town. It was a big city with small town networks among the wealthy.

When the trial regarding Gary's firm was a few weeks off, the firm staved it off and fought to get it dropped on legal grounds and every other way they could.

"When I was in the trenches in Korea I heard incoming shells," Gary told me. "Quiet at first, kind of a loud whistling noise getting louder and louder as it drew nearer. As they got louder, it scared the hell out of me wondering if it was going to land on us. This fucking trial coming up is like that, a quiet whistle but getting louder and louder wondering if it's going to blow up on me and the firm."

Somehow, I understood the kind of fear he was experiencing. He had been the hot attorney in this part of town for a long time and he had some famous and lucrative cases.

As it turns out, my old employer in the tall building overlooking the bay was also remotely involved in the J David fiasco. I remember notes by my desk in a box on the floor that was already there when I started working at the company. There were notes on J David and some of the firms involved in the legal ramifications. When I saw what it was, I stopped looking and handed the notes to his assistant. She destroyed them immediately.

It was just an amazing story that involved the most influential people in the highest places. The Mayor of San Diego and other politicians I knew were touched by J David and his huge money scheme.

Even J David's PR agent was beyond reproach, having been a big Kahuna in the power structure of the town, his big house with its big mortgage was paid by J David and he was not questioning anything.

You can be walking down the road minding your own business and the law can just whack you in the rear. So many people believe that if you just do the right thing you will never have a problem with the law. People watch too much television. It is not always the bad guy who gets whacked by the legal system.

The trial of Gary's firm came up and I attended some of it. J David was in jail already doing his time for his part in the Ponzi schemes. Gary was called to the stand and asked his version of what the renegade partner had done. As he was recalling what he could, the columnist that I was bringing up yelled, "You are lying!" from the gallery in the middle of Gary's testimony. So much for the objectivity of the press.

I knew he was not lying but I did not want to add to the chaos of the trial. After that day's session, I called the court asking for any news and the judge just happened to answer. I was shocked and he could tell I was shocked that I had reached him.

"The columnist was wrong," I told him.

"I understand your concern," the judge said.

I never told him my name for fear of interference with justice or some such. I have no idea if the judge believed me or not but I know the judge was later found to have been taking bribes from certain attorneys coming in front of his bench. So out the window goes any thought I ever had about how clean the legal structure is and how things are stable and true to their purpose. No institution or social system is stable, pure, or true as long as people are involved and when you strip them down to their bare reality, people is all they are made of.

Gary did not like the way the trial was going and was angry with the defending attorney who had been hired by the insurance company out of Los Angeles. I could tell that things were not going well in the trial and the high-powered defense attorney seemed to be biding his time and collecting his money. Gary was one guy who knew what should have been going on but there was little he could do: the insurance company was paying for it and everyone knows that "a lawyer who defends himself has a fool for a client." As a lawyer defending yourself, you cannot see past your own self-interest and ego. You are more than likely to look past legal procedure, theory to show how the other party is wrong, thereby burying yourself with your own shovel.

Gary once complained to me that, "His Company bought him a new God damn Rolls Royce for collecting a $4000 an hour fee from our insurance company. It sure as hell is not a prize for the job he is doing in the courtroom for us. He comes into court wearing Armani suits and a Rolex. He is pissing them all off in that court."

Gary came into the office with his brand of humor one morning. "They have to use white rats instead of lawyers for research animals." Gary said.

Taking the bait I asked why this was so.

"Because white rats don't screw each other in the ass constantly," he said, smiling.

The trial dragged on and those in the firm were for the most part cognizant of the end game. The judge ruled that Gary and his firm were "aiding and abetting" J David and his Ponzi scheme and awarded the investors over $500,000 in damages. This was a lot of money in that day. Gary came back to the offices and put together a statement of his own in reaction to the court's decision.

Another partner of the firm asked me to "just let him deal with the loss in his own way." I sat in Gary's office waiting for him to scribble it all out and make copies of his press release. It was mostly sour grapes in its tone and hard for me to take seriously. It was more a rant than a statement. I suppose he wanted me to distribute this thing but he never asked me to and I never offered. I did not know it yet but that was to have been our last meeting. He let me know by hinting that he was retiring from the legal industry to write and become a photographer. The Monday after the trial, I gave Gary a call at the office and was told he was not expected to come in. He never returned to his office. He had cleaned out his desk on that prior day when he had told me of his plan to travel the world and photograph beach people. I have not seen him since that day of the end of the trial. That last day I saw him he gave me his usual farewell by saluting me and blurting out, "I'll SUE ya!"

Chapter Six

THE WILD MEN OF COMMERCIAL DEVELOPMENT

Under the Guise of Order and Management

As we experienced the prosperity that comes with being the first time the city hosted an NFL Super Bowl, my company was also flourishing as we rode the wave of major real estate development. During that Super Bowl, the temperature across the entire country was 30 degrees or lower, with the exception of Southern California. We were experiencing a Santa Ana, whereby a high-pressure area develops over the desert forcing hot winds through the mountains and to the cities along the Pacific Ocean. We were enjoying temperatures in the 80s and the televised images of our warm bay and palm trees, sailboats and beautiful people frolicking on our beaches was not missed by the freezing miserable masses to the east.

Developers of real estate everywhere noted this lucrative phenomenon. We had professional firms setting up shop from all over the country: law firms, accounting firms, architects, all there to take advantage of the situation. The largest of these were the commercial and residential developers. A developer from Florida called me about a high-end parking garage he and his partner were going to build. He wanted me to mastermind a promotional strategy for his garage that would somehow bypass any problems with government red tape and the city council. In addition to the structure's expansive space for expensive cars, it would offer a car detail service that would clean every crevice and crack in your car until it sparkled, making the driver look like they must be somebody. Kind of a goofy idea, but it fit the times. Maybe it still does.

It just so happened that prior to starting my company, I volunteered to work with a popular member of the city council. In fact, I had actually attended a special award banquet that she'd thrown for me where I was unaware of its purpose and quite surprised. I'd personally walked precincts with this candidate, who often asked for my advice on strategy since I had worked for another popular candidate when he ran for president years before.

While walking precincts we would pick a spot on a map within her precinct and, from time to time, ended up in places we should not have been. Once, while in a very seedy area, we started knocking doors and passing out brochures heralding the wonderful things the candidate would accomplish for the voters. We'd even throw in a word or two about doing away with the problems inherent to the universe for good measure.

I will never forget this small house in the middle of a lot, kind of off by itself. It looked alright so I knocked on the door with the city office candidate beside me. Thinking I heard someone inside, I knocked again. This time I heard a clicking noise that sounded like a door opening from the back of the house. We looked towards the side of the house in time to see a pit bull running straight toward us. Someone had actually let this evil creature out to devour us. As a dog person, I can tell by the disposition of a dog if it is actually going to tear you open or if it just wants to scare you. This dog was one mean son of a bitch and he was hell bent on killing both of us. He ran toward me with little hesitation and I knew if I turned to run it would be like putting a steak on my face yelling, "Kill me!" Without a weapon, my only defense was to act as though I was not afraid to face him. As I turned toward him, he did slow a bit - just enough to allow me to back up 10 feet to my car. I quickly opened the door and got in, noticing the candidate was already in the car waiting.

"Thanks for being my decoy for that dog," she said breathlessly. "You might have even saved my life." For some sick reason we found ourselves laughing.

That was the last of the precinct walks for that day.

However, it gave me an open door at the council and I knew what the drift was on a project like this high-end garage. I had my assistant approach the planning department and gain as much knowledge as she could on the parking garage.

This was an aggressive move, to actually walk into the city planning department and ask directly about the property very much impressed my client from Florida. It scared the hell out of his partner though. He yelled and screamed at us about how we would kill the project with this kind of maneuver, ruin both he and his marriage, and put him into bankruptcy. His screams, couched in the worst profanity allowed by tongue, mouth, lung, raging and shouting, freaking everyone in the room out of their wits.

It takes a while to calm oneself down after such a demonstration. It takes gallons of Old Overcoat brandy and 10 hours of meditation near the gentle waves of the sea to regain sanity after being chewed out like that. In the end, the person who had hired us and signed the contract was happy. He handed us big checks and we got over the incident quite quickly.

The aim of the city was to eliminate parking downtown forcing the populace to use public transportation. The city council thought that less parking would make the city modern and earth friendly and commercially more attractive to tourists. The city father's brought in a major developer who shared their vision of eliminating parking downtown. Planning a designing things Disneyland-style. My work was cut out for me, so I had to hit the media hard and fast to convince the "powers that be" that they should let my client's parking project pass. My objective in getting the OK from the council was to present it as a place that needed more parking, not less thus making the place available to the local visitor as well.

As the city council voted to eliminate much of the parking downtown, I wrote an op-ed piece about how the city was going to squeeze business out of the developing part of downtown that was just coming into its own economically. Because I could not very well sign my name to the article, I placed a call to a major property owner in that area to see if he would sign his name to it as the writer. He did it in a flash. He was proud of the controversy and relished the attention he got from city leaders. The article discussed how similar attempts in other cities were an economic failure. That writing was placed in the major newspaper on a Sunday. Another op-ed I wrote was placed on page 1 of an important local news media paper looking like a real news item, thanks to a lazy reporter. This was but one more assault on the idea of less parking. We placed more articles and opinion pieces as though written by people having political influence. This was what we needed for the idea to take on its own momentum. The city council voted unanimously to pass the permit for the parking structure and the night they did I told my client of the good news. They were convinced we walked on water but we knew we had just passed out the kool-aid.

My firm by now was rated among the "Top 10 Best" list of Public Relations firms in Southern California. Business was easier to procure and we attracted more and more new clients.

Over time, I became complacent and far too confident in my presentation skills. I had, in the early days of my firm, seen proposals presented by competitors that were appallingly bad. Proposing things like putting a "communications fence" around your real estate for sale, as if potential clients would believe you come to them with a magic wand and unfathomable powers to do anything you wish in the media. It was as though a PR firm could just snap their fingers and place their clients' market position in a private magazine. Yes, such a thing is possible but it takes time and cultivation of relationships. It was as though the task of PR is to influence publishers to forget about receiving big bucks for advertising and insert your clients' wonders instead.

Competitors proposed impossible tasks knowing it would never happen. Those proposed tasks look great to the potential sucker (aka client) but such proposals built the expectation that all of the PR firms would offer the same no matter how lame or impossible. The one thing I thought I had learned was to be more realistic with my proposals because I did not want to promise what could not be delivered. I wanted to promise less and deliver more than expected. That had worked well for my company, at least so far.

The developer's partner, who had screamed and chewed me and my company out, was now so impressed he invited me to handle marketing for a major downtown high-rise he was developing. He informed me that there were three other investors in on the project, so I would have to give a formal presentation on what I would do marketing-wise. This was just for show, this presentation of our proposal, he said with a wink, as I already had the account.

As I said before, I was feeling complacent and as I formulated a proposal, I left out all the hype-induced programs that not even God could pull off, let alone a PR firm. Bad idea. These potential clients had heard so many proposals with these grand ideas that my proposal likely looked short in comparison. It was too realistic.

The partner asked me to meet him at his headquarters in the morning where he and his partners on the project would be entertaining proposals from contractors to build the high rise. I arrived on time at 11:30AM. What I had not counted on was that they had been hearing proposals all morning and were wearily looking forward to lunch.

The partner asked, "Why don't you come to lunch with us and we could hear your proposal then?"

A little voice in my head told me never to give a proposal over lunch, but I was stuck so I had to say said yes. I could not turn him down now. People chomping on sandwiches and sipping wine are not likely to give you their undivided attention. Presentations should always be scheduled for a time when all parties are focused on the task. During lunch is not that time. Worse, it is neigh-on impossible to talk and eat at the same time without slobbering your food. There is too much attention paid to eating and trying to look professional while proposing your ideas, crumbs hanging on your teeth, mustard rolling off your lips. But what the heck, I already had this one in the bag so I could make a few mistakes. Or so I thought.

The investing partners slowly came out of the conference room, all bleary-eyed, tired, and hungry for lunch. And I was going to pitch them.

"Why was there such a spread between proposals?" The partner asked to the others as they emerged. "There was a $20M spread between the highest and the lowest bid."

I was searching for an answer that would show them my financial prowess and superior knowledge of all things high-rise and contractor related - but I came up with nothing.

Just then, one of the administrative assistants told the partner he had a phone call. He took the call and listened as his face grew an odd shade of purple. He was getting angry at whatever news came from the other end of the telephone.

"WHAT?" he yelled into the phone. "HE DID WHAT?" Several seconds went by. "YOU TELL THAT MOTHER FUCKER I AM GOING TO FUCKING SUE HIS ASS FOR EVERYTHING HE HAS!" He screamed, slamming the receiver down so hard it broke into two pieces.

Note to self, do not give a proposal during lunch to people who have spent grueling hours hearing contractor minutia, followed by really bad news that turns them into wild-assed apes.

As we walked out of the office, my inviter stood fuming, waiting for the elevator. I cracked some stupid joke, I forget about what, that did not help alleviate the situation at all.

We walked outside the building towards a delicatessen while they mostly talked about the proposals for the 50-story multi-million dollar building. They ordered their sandwiches and sat discussing the hotels where they were staying. They finally gave me something of a notice to start, which was nice of them, so I started my story as best I could under the circumstances. I got about half way through, noticing these people were all trying their best not to fall asleep. I was pitching to myself. I plodded on knowing this was wasted time. Finally, the partner asked to talk to me alone, so we walked over to the salad bar.

He asked, "Why didn't you talk about a communications fence around the city by placing articles in airline magazines?"

I knew he had talked to other companies like mine at that point. I could not say, "Because it is just so much crap and PR proposal hype." Somehow, that did not seem a good thing to say to a person who was loaded with sandwich and had just come down off a crazy man high. We returned and sat down in time to hear one of the investors say, "we just build it and watch the buyer shark frenzy" as though buyers would be dying to buy in. When the building was finished, it received some bad reviews from the *L.A. Times* and a major real estate recession had begun. There was no frenzy and no sharks.

It was the great white elephant downtown and remained mostly empty for years. They made some obvious mistakes on the place. It was an odd dark color next to a beautiful bay and did not fit in well with its environment. There was a lot of anticipation about the first floor having upscale retail shops and grand restaurants, yet the plan discouraged any kind of foot traffic. Foot traffic was allowed at the building by Valet parking only. How much clientele did they think they would receive with a plan like that? Bad planning, no marketing and a failed project go hand-in-hand.

I asked my developer if he would be interested in a proposal I had for a new restaurant at the place. This was during the concept stage of the high-rise and in my naivety, I gave him a proposal for a great restaurant with no cost numbers, no expected customer base, nothing except some remedies for things I hate most about restaurants. It would have all sound-attenuating booths and no tables next to swinging kitchen doors. The ground floor would be granite and the two floors above would be glass so everyone could see everyone else. The stairs up to the high levels would also be glass. Walls would be sound absorbing, because I hate noisy restaurants. I like a wide-open look in a restaurant. I do not think he so much as responded to my (not) well thought-out proposal. His lack of response spoke volumes and he was right, even though he may not have known it. A restaurant needs traffic and people to actually eat there. If you can only get to the place by car then there is no line waiting to get in to savor whatever you have to serve. No people waiting outside of a new restaurant means no buzz on the street as to how popular or cool it is.

But my big mistake in that proposal was the lack of numbers and marketing. Pretty strange for a marketer. Sometimes we just do not know what we do not know.

The building was finally constructed and so was the high-end parking garage. Then the recession started so my Florida developer went back to where he came from and so did other professional firms. The local partner, whom I had given that horrible proposal to, went on to the next big thing in California - technology.

I worked with several other developers and came away realizing that they are a rare group. They are not so much managers as they are motivators and influencers, motivated for the big bucks one gets by building something truly desirable, then selling it to the highest bidder. Commercial real estate is built by people who drag highly talented crews into their tent and use them to death, while making sure they get large sums of money. Not many people could do what they do and still feel human.

II TECHNOLOGY

Chapter Seven

THE MEETING MONSTER AND THE UGLY DUCKLINGS

I have always been a student of all things technical - from the innards of a clock to playing with software as a wannabe code developer. Having taught computer classes, I prefer to believe I know more about computers in general than most others. One of my first jobs at a technical company was as a public relations consultant on marketing high-tech products. To respect their privacy, I will refer to this tech company as Inter Computer Advantage (ICA). I interviewed with the VP of Marketing and gave her my best PR-tech spiel. She was quite taken with my background and my work as a consultant.

As a professor of law, I am familiar with certain legal requirements regarding a company relationship with an independent contractor. Since the company does not pay taxes on behalf of an independent contractor, there are certain laws that the company must abide by. However, few companies seem to understand what those laws are, setting themselves up for pain in a court of law.

The VP talked to me about her expectations and it became clear she wanted me to be physically in the office from 8:00AM to 5:00PM, just like the other employees who had their taxes paid by the company and receiving benefits, health insurance and paid vacations. She said she'd provide me with an office and a computer, then told me what my first project would look like. This went against all legal guidelines for an independent contractor. In fact, when it was time for me to pay my taxes I could argue in a court of law that the company should pay. The law states that when a company hires an independent contractor, that contractor and company must sign an agreement as to which party will pay for the contractor's federal and state taxes. If the new hire is a contractor then the contractor pays tax on income. There should be an agreement clearly stating what the company expects from the contractor, outlining all deliverables and what the end product should look like. The company cannot lay down restrictions or guidelines as to how the contractor will achieve these expectations. The company will not tell the contractor what hours they must hold or furnish tools or a place to work. If these things are in place the contractor is not a contractor but an employee and must be provided all benefits.

Not caring at the time, I agreed to her conditions. The one thing I must have, I told her, was my own office so I could make phone calls to editors. A PR person cannot be taken seriously by a *Wall Street Journal* editor if it sounds like they are some small time hustler in a noisy boiler room.

From day one, I sensed that things were just not right. I was shuffled off to a cubicle (rather than an office as promised) right after I met with human resources for reasons that were never very clear. Nothing there ever became clear. The VP told me that the company was a "reboot," as most employees were new hires since the old company did not do well. That worried me right off the bat, but I took solace in the fact that I was not an actual employee. The first thing I was asked to do was attend a meeting my VP had scheduled. There were several people at this meeting, including two very young girls whose jobs I never fully understood. The meeting kicked off by revealing several large, homemade posters designed to display our products in an artistic way. The posters were a poor attempt by a graphics artist to intertwine industrial technology (heavy-duty industrial drop-proof computers) with rich consumers living the high life in their tennis gear while sipping wine. I was having trouble wrapping my brain around the concept, but I was sure it would come to me later. There was no agenda for the meeting and no action items were assigned. We just sat around the table while the VP led us in a gabfest. I was sure when lunchtime rolled around that she would dismiss us from that bore of a get together. However, when lunchtime rolled around there was a knock on the door and in came a person carrying a sack of boxed lunches. The VP opened the boxes, pulled out a bunch of sandwiches and placed them on paper plates for us to choose from. There were soft drinks packed in ice for us as well. Here we were accomplishing nothing, listening to pointless rants on unrelated topics seemingly sprung out of her imagination, yet this was considered such an important meeting that we were not even getting out for lunch!

Another hour or two went by like this, where we were unable to leave for the bathroom or escape to our stinking cubicle. This was a sign of things to come.

I might have been able to limp along with a cubicle if it had some kind of soundproofing, but it was not even a private cube, at that. The two young girls from the meeting shared this space with me. They sat making phone calls to friends and doing their nails, but mostly they talked to each other in high-pitched teen tones, yelping the day away. Except when they were busy kissing the VP's ass.

As the days passed, these two girls spent less and less time in the cubicle and more and more time with the VP, doing who knows what. Reading through tons of company documentation, struggling for a point to be taken from it all, I began wondering what I was supposed to be doing here. My VP scheduled meeting after meeting, marking my attendance as mandatory, filling up every day of my calendar with meetings, so the day was filled with meaningless meetings and any actual accomplishment was just a distant memory.

As it turns out, this woman was from Hewlett Packard. A huge company like that is a big bureaucracy. It is full of departments with dictators at the top, each jealously guarding their position in the scheme of the corporation.

These department heads looked busy and important to the people they reported to, and there is no better way to look like you are doing important things then having constant meetings and taking important calls from the boss. Meetings provide an aura of reality and importance but unless real activity is put into action, they are worthless for everyone attending. And it does nothing for the company's bottom line. I thought back to the need for an agenda and no meetings over one hour.

Eventually I just stopped attending these meetings and started developing something of a plan I would present to my VP. As I worked on it, she would swish by me with her two girls following close behind like a couple of ducklings waddling behind Momma Duck. Working here seemed mostly impossible and quite surreal. The boss was not a serious contender for any meaningful attention nor was she concerned about anything like production. I could never figure out what she accomplished or what value she gave to the company… outside of talking to people in meetings. This not only described her, but other new hires in the place, like me. It is very hard to be effective if effective people do not surround you. There seemed to be a variety of managers hired from Hewlett Packard who spent a lot of time talking to each other about nothing. I could not see anything her two ducklings were doing outside of talking to mother duck about more stuff and junk.

I tried connecting directly with one of the engineers who was supposedly developing products for the company. He came up with rugged disk drives and chassis to put the drives in for rugged use in manufacturing. This made sense. I thought it might be the outlet I was looking for. This engineer was at least 300 lbs and maybe 5'7.

He was never without a two-quart plastic bottle of Classic Coke. I wrote a few lines good for an internal newsletter for him and was told to route it through several people whom I had never heard of to this point. I did so and received not a single piece of feedback or commentary from anyone. As near as I could tell, this company had not been successful at much of anything and someone or some board had gutted most of what they had in terms of talent, assuming that by injecting a new set of people from big companies it would be a success. I was only at that company for one month, never receiving a clue as to what its vision or mission was or where it seemed to be going. I was never sure it had, nor did I ever see, a product in the place. The company ceases to exist today and I suspect it might have been someone's write-off, as it had to be a major source of cash incineration. Any one of those meetings had to be paying each employee an average of $100 an hour. With a meeting of 10, that was about $1000 an hour wasted during those meetings with other such meeting going on around the building at the same time. I never found out what happened to mother duck and her ducklings. I did learn the value of efficiency in meetings.

Chapter Eight

The inventors of all things technical.

I landed a gig at a high-tech company that was a spin-off of a major Department of a Defense contractor. I was privileged to be at this company as the new Marketing Guru and techno-geek when it invented an advanced cable modem chipset still used today by consumers when they access the Internet, cable television and other breakthrough technologies. I was involved in many aspects of these inventions on the ground level, not realizing the impact they would have on society.

One of my tasks was developing marketing plans for products the engineers had conjured up. They developed a single chip for cable modems that could handle digital data, audio, and video signals - functions that were currently performed by four to six chips. That same month we unveiled an interactive digital television (DTV) set-top box (STB) platform. Another invention from this company was the birth of TiVo, which found its story on 60 Minutes. We created a product that delivered stable Voice over Internet Protocol (VOIP) and the ability to talk over the Internet.

Pure success all day, every day. The culture was mostly happy and cheerful, jokes flying and a lot of backslapping, elbow patting and hand shaking among the inmates. We had offices all over the world and I was involved in everything from writing white papers introducing products and their potential, to managing major trade show events demonstrating these products to potential customers.

Trade shows tend to be a bragging place for a company to anyone who will listen. They help build the personae of a company and make it recognizable to the world through branding. The cable modem chip, for example, was presented at a major trade show in Chicago. I was in charge of designing brochures, producing and presenting them at the event, booking hotel rooms and meeting rooms large enough to present the product to companies such as AT&T. We had our prospects picked up in a limousine and taken to the presentation.

We presented ourselves as a tech company on the same level as anyone from Silicon Valley, which we were. Everyone wanted to look the part of Steve Jobs in his garage, working alongside Wozniak with the T-shirt and jeans. As an employee, you knew that if a person was walking down our hallowed halls in a suit that they had to be a salesperson or interviewing for a job. While coordinating people for this major trade show, I received a call from a couple of fellows from one of our acquisitions on the East Coast.

When these fellows came to our California offices, they always wore suits, which was simply a difference in business culture between the East and West Coasts. One of them suggested to me that everyone should wear suits to the show to demonstrate professionalism. That seemed like a good idea so I emailed a memo to everyone attending the show telling them to wear suits. I did not anticipate so much flack over it. Our Senior VP called me and said, "That's not who we are. Issue another directive and tell everyone to dress like they work for a tech company in a T-shirt and jeans."

I could hardly believe it. I surmised this as the end of the "Mad Men" look in American business.

Developing literature here was not like doing so for a non-technical product. I sat in on all the engineering meetings regarding the development of these new products where ideas would bloom. For example, the creation of an on-demand Internet telephone service for business that supported an unlimited number of lines. This allowed users to simply pick up the phone and a line would appear as if by Internet magic.

A great lesson in management came to me from these meetings and by observing the way the company was structured. The senior vice president of marketing was a British engineer , an engineer who was comfortable as a marketer or a marketer comfortable as an engineer, I am not sure. The prior tech company I had experience with had strict division between the engineering and marketing department. Even worse, the marketing department was separate from the public relations department. Departments had evolved separately and had no cohesion of effort or common thought whatsoever. There was no synergy there and they struggled against one another for relevance.

This company, however, fostered an interesting culture where anything and everything seemed not only possible but also inevitable. The culprit lurking around the corner was the end of our type of chip and its use in the computer modem that was common to the dial up Internet connection. Everyone knew our time was limited. Our bread and butter was the chip used in most technical communication devices such as the soon-to-be popular cell phone, the fax machine (remember those?), the dial up modem used to access the Internet via telephone lines, the wireless landline and many basic computer functions.

At that establishment and time, management was mostly relegated to sweating and fretting over how we could deliver more product than we had on hand and how much to produce before it was all considered on the dinosaur shelf no longer in demand. Tech devices and inventions were obsolete in the face of new evolutionary products, replacing old ones almost on a daily basis. Everyone in the company knew this so the object was to strike while the iron was hot. When I joined the company, its price per share was $16. When I left, it was $125. After that, it spun off several companies, was eventually bought by a San Francisco tech enterprise, and is no longer public.

There were meetings but no more than two or three a week. Seldom did these meetings meet for more than an hour and they always had a specific point. We had one major companywide meeting every two weeks where all of the employees involved in management assembled in a large room. It was at these meetings that control took place.

An example of this was when a department head got up on stage to give the other managers a product status update and announced when the next level of development would be ready. One such manager got up and talked about a project that was three weeks late in its progress. When that kind of lag takes place, it puts the other departments in a bind as they are waiting their turn to move on that project. One-by-one each department manager who was being held up stood and grilled the guy on stage as to the progress of his project and what was holding it up. In this case, the manager begged for more time and the attending vice president gave it to him much to the chagrin of the others. Peer pressure works as the best manager of all. He was the goat of the moment and the others had let him know it all in civilized and respectful tones. No bad mouthing, no name-calling, and no blaming took place and it was quite efficient.

My boss, the easy going happy Englishman (who was having an affair with his secretary) held meetings each week in his office and covered subjects such as how the arrangements were coming for the trade show or how to brand a new product or some other detail. He was an intelligent engineer and knew how to deal with office politics. If one of his people badmouthed another, he would let the other know somehow such as forwarding a negative email or voicemail to the person being badmouthed. Everyone knew that badmouthing a fellow employee would get back to him or her. A very effective way to keep poison politics out of the office.

So is it management or is it just the situation that makes things work? Creating an environment where the employees are smart and happy with an emphasis on products sought after by markets, sometimes when markets themselves do not know they want the product, works. An upbeat culture and sense of future and accomplishment are very difficult to teach or to find in a management class are elements common to success. In most management textbooks, it is as though all these things are already in place. There is so much involved in an environment of business it would seem overwhelming to try to understand it, but time and temperament are the keys to understanding and making it work.

III FINANCE

Chapter Nine

The shell game - TXC

There is a great deal of mystery around public companies and the process involved in becoming one. A startup company may consist of one person developing and producing a particular type of product, be it a technological breakthrough or a simple revision of some product making it more attractive or useful. That one-person company may grow to employ hundreds of people years later.

As the sole proprietor, a one-person owner might have a small but profitable company but be liable for a legal suit. If some degree of protection against personal liability is desired, the company may take on a corporate or Limited Liability legal structure. This legal structure might look like a corporation based and owned by shares, each share being some portion of value of the company. These shares may be owned by anyone. As an example, if the entire worth of a company equals $1000, there might be 10 shares worth $100 each. The founder of the company could own all the shares or a co-founder might own half. If one person owns more than 50 percent of all the shares, they are entitled to run the company but none of the shareholders is liable for company wrong doing.

The limited liability company (LLC), offers the same protection from being sued on a personal basis as does the corporation. At some point, a company might be large and profitable enough that the managers will want to take it to the next level. The next level has become one of those catchy but overused concepts that means someone wants to make the company larger and more profitable based on some subjective standard. What this means to many business owners is taking a company "public."

Taking a company public means offering shares of a company to the general public to purchase for however much the investors are willing to pay. The shares must be offered on a legal market or platform such as the New York Stock Exchange, the NASDAQ, Bulletin Board and the like . Since there is a lot of room for graft and fraud in this market, the process to become a public company is a long, hard, legal and tedious task. It is a process full of red tape and legal movement. It is difficult and the books must be open for inspection to be sure the company is legitimate and has financial stability to protect any member of the public who buys shares of the company once it becomes public.

Why go public? Companies go public because of the "Market Capitalization." If the public is willing to pay $200 for a share worth $100 there is a "market cap" of $200 per share. We now have the money necessary to go to the next level.

There is, however, a way to get a public company that has gone through the difficult process whereby a buyer of a company does not have to prove finances or fill out any forms. It is called a "corporate shell." A corporate shell is a company that is officially public as far as the government is concerned but has no employees, products, buildings or tangible evidence of its existence, yet might have been in its past a legitimate corporation. It is perfectly legal and may be bought as a ready-made public company, which the buyer can insert product or service into and be on a trade list for the public to buy its shares. Many of these are on the Over the Counter Bulletin Board (OTCBB), also known as "pink sheets" stock. These are mostly under the radar of the Securities and Exchange Commission (SEC), making it easier to manipulate the price.

During my early years as a naive stock trader, I looked into several stock message boards of legitimate companies. Occasionally on a real company stock message board, someone would post something like "TXC is on fire, get in fast!"

Out of sheer curiosity, I would go to the message board where this stock was being discussed. One such stock (I have changed the letters a bit, as there are lawsuits still in motion over this, among many others) was TXC. It was interesting to watch the back-and-forth banter on the message board. Several individuals posted several times every day. They made it seem as though they had inside information as to what was going on in the company, and even posted news releases on the message board. I found an original message board with the first news releases. These releases, shown below, have been censored for legal purposes but the content thrust has not been changed.

NEWS RELEASE

T.com, Inc. forecasts a 150 Percent Revenue Increase in Q1; Company Exceeds Half-Million Dollars in Current Quarter Monthly Billing

Business Wire - August 04, 1999 08:38

OAKLAND, Calif.--(BUSINESS WIRE)--Aug. 4—T.com, Inc. (OTC BB:TXC), today reported monthly billings for July 1-July 31 exceeded $575,000, **representing an approximated 150 percent increase for the current quarter's revenue projection, over the Q4 revenue postings.**

This represents a 404 percent increase in the current quarter's monthly revenue base over the previous quarter's monthly revenue postings. The company forecasted significant earning potential for their first quarter in their fourth quarter financial results released July 29, 1999, citing both expansion of their pre-paid and one plus customer billing and centralized operational management.

When asked about the company's reported growth and profitability, T.com president and CEO stated, "We are following our plan and driving this Company to meet and exceed its revenue forecasts and projections. Consider for a minute what we have reported in the last ninety days alone, not only have we entered into a number of lucrative and beneficial strategic alliances we have aligned ourselves with experienced marketing partners to properly and efficiently promote our products and services. In doing so, we have added more marketing muscle to our overall strategy and increased our profitability exponentially."

The company's revenue forecasts take into consideration all new distribution and contract expansion agreements previously reported and anticipated to yield in excess of $40 million in annualized revenue.

The company has also announced a number of strategic alliances during the last 90 days expanding their international calling network, which is expected to significantly increase international transport revenue opportunities for the company.

As a fully reporting telecommunications and Internet marketing company, this dotcom has been in operation for more than 14 years, specializing in pre-paid telecommunication, one-plus long distance, and telephonic and Internet based lottery participation. The company officially changed its name on May 17, reflecting its progression and focus into Internet marketing and E-commerce. This was to promote and market its pre-paid telecommunications products and services, including the innovative HitLoTTo(R) Club Card.

Sounds good, doesn't it? The good news kept on coming, at least on the still active message board. Below are more messages that have been censored.

Tuesday May 25, 09:04 AM Eastern time
Company Press Release

Group V Stockholders Seek Increased Holdings -- Shareholders Approach Company to Purchase Restricted Shares

SAN FRANCISCO--(BUSINESS WIRE)--May 25, 1999— company, Inc. (OTC BB:TXC), formerly S Corporation, reported today that several major shareholders have elected to increase their share holdings in the company. Accordingly, the company has agreed to sell at market price, two million, six hundred eight thousand two hundred ninety-one (2,608,291) restricted shares of common stock.

The announcement follows the May 7, 1999, report of the company's President and Chairman purchasing six million shares of restricted common stock.

The company has recently reported sizable pre-paid phone card contracts and plans for a consolidation of its subsidiary operations which is expected to increase product margins and profitability within the next quarter.

The company's President and Chairman, Joseph M. was quoted as saying, "Considering the company's promising future and expanding revenue opportunities, I am not surprised to find our shareholders eager to increase their holdings." Mr. M. added, "These new shares will be restricted under rule 144 and cannot be sold for two years. Certainly our shareholders have faith in our ability to build additional revenue and maintain solid growth in upcoming quarters." The proceeds of this sale will be used as additional working capital to accelerate the company's business plan and stock buy back program.

During the recent quarter, the company's focus has expanded to include vertical markets that have integrated Internet based transaction and E-commerce activities to support the company's sales and marketing strategies.

T.com, Inc. (a publicly traded company OTC BB:TXC) is a diversified telecommunications company specializing in some of the world's most profitable market segments including one plus, toll free long distance and pre-paid phone card products.

Forward-looking statements in this release are made pursuant to the "safe harbor" provisions of the Private Securities Litigation Reform Act of 1995. Investors are cautioned that such forward-looking statements involve risks and uncertainties, including, without limitation, continued acceptance of the Company's products, increased levels of competition for the Company, new products and technological changes, the Company's dependence upon third-party suppliers, intellectual property rights and other risks detailed from time to time in the Company's periodic reports filed with the Securities and Exchange Commission.

Today, the company president has bought millions of shares and shareholders are clamoring to buy more. A business plan will be accelerated, a stock buyback is mentioned. When stock is bought, it goes up. Sounds like a very good company to get into. Constant drumming and more posters coming into the fray on the message board saw constant information like the following:

$.65! What a BUYING OPPORTUNITY!

With the broad-based early morning sell-off TXC has dropped 35% from yesterday's close. Will not last long. Those who were "asleep" yesterday have another shot to buy shares <$1 this morning.

What a bargain this market has given us...

You get the picture. The price showed a start of pennies per share, which is why it is called a penny stock, then with lots of hype on the message board it rose to about a $1.50 a share. There was never a product or a service and all the news was made up in these scammer's heads.

A lawsuit was finally filed by the SEC some 10 years later, due to the continual defrauding through many other fake companies by these same people. Two executives are serving time in jail and our CEO quoted above was ruled to pay back $3M to investors. You can bet he swindled many more millions than that over time. He and his friends were generating fake invoices to show revenues of millions according to the suit against them by the SEC.

There is apparently a way to buy stock through Europe and the American SEC will not notice large volume activity on the stock if the stock is sold in huge amounts at a time.

Once the price approached a $1.50, the stock dropped to almost zero. The scammers who owned the shell owned lots of the stock at pennies then sold the stock for millions through foreign brokers. Many of the investors on the board bought shares with their life savings, some even borrowed against their house to buy this stock. It was a scam through and through and the people who set it up and exaggerated its worth seemed to have gotten away with it and would have, had they stopped with this one scam. Once I detected it was a scam, I called the SEC office in Los Angeles. The attorney who took my call listened intently as I gave him the story about what was going on.

He responded with an audible sigh then said, "You know, I get phone calls like this all the time. It sounds like it could involve millions but we are very much overloaded here. I am covering all of Southern California and there are two of us here. We concentrate on the biggest frauds as a priority. We are doing what we can to deal with those in the billions."

I was shocked. To me it meant that this was not the only such fraud going on. The Internet was new to users at this point and people tended to see a message board as credible even though what people said on it was not always true. This was the new technology producing a new flavor of crime. You buy a shell company, putting it on the pink sheets on the Over the Counter (OTC) exchange and then you have people go to other message boards and tell them of your shell company's message board and how great the company is doing. Then you have your shills pump the stock, talk about how great it is and how it is growing and how, as an investor, you need to get in. When the price of the stock is up from being bought, you dump your shares for a profit. It is called "pump and dump" for a reason and is a favorite tactic in the world of finance. It takes many forms in the industry. I had not had that much experience yet as trader or investor so this was a revelation. Frauds were everywhere and people were getting away with it big time. The TXC scam and many other such bogus OTC companies were taking advantage of the new technology. There is little doubt this are still rampant in many forms.

My Education as a Stock Trader

I used my hard-earned money to buy and sell stocks on a regular basis. When I began, there was no such concept as a day trader. To buy and sell you had to hook your computer up to an 800 number to buy or sell stock on the markets. The practice of buying and selling on the Internet was not yet perfected.

Information and data on the stock market was not as readily available as it is now. Trading in the stock market was like feeling your way down a dark tunnel. Brokers online were new to the game and that was where you found your information on a stock. There was no CNBC or any good way to get information outside of what the brokers allowed you to see. Trading involves a lot of luck now but even more then. I bought databases through the mail on floppy disks with information about the universe of stocks offered and I was able to manipulate that data to find attractive stocks. The information was days old, whereas today information is available instantly. I usually bought the stock that gained value rapidly over time within its industry.

One such stock, which was of a company that produced technological material, seemed on fire. I bought it at about $5 per share. The company reported its earnings for each quarter, as do all public companies. A pattern was evolving with this company. Each quarter it would report great earnings and the stock would shoot up by about $15 a share. All one had to do to make money was get in before earnings were announced and sell after the announcement. It was clear to me that many other traders were doing this because you could see it gradually rise in price as earning announcements came near. I made a ton of money on this particular stock. At one earnings report, I sold my investment in it and made a profit of $32,000. That was the most money I had ever made in an hour.

I began to think like a gambler, becoming bolder with my moves soon harboring delusional thinking of things like the difference between small returns and large returns based on where the decimal point was in the numbers. Why not trade big numbers with the decimal point farther to the right and make the big bucks?

I bet the farm as they say, on the next earnings report from this company. I watched the stock price edge up during that previous day. My feet began to get cold so I put in a sell order at 49 and one quarter per share just before the end of trading. This was one eighth of a dollar over what would have sold it at, an immediate sell. I was much too greedy to let that extra eighth per share pass. The next morning at 6AM, the report was out. The CEO of that company added the statement "we cannot continue in the future with the pace of revenues we have realized in the past."

All hell broke loose and the shares began to sell off. I fired up my computer, got into my brokerage on the 800 number, and got in line to sell. Technology these days allows you to sell instantly but technology then forced you to get in line. By the time my turn came, I had lost $250,000. It ruined my day to say the least. It was a hard lesson to learn. It was at that point that I understood what is meant by "bears make money and bulls make money but pigs get slaughtered."

Chapter Ten

BEWARE THE PROFESSIONAL MONEY MANAGER

Financial Management

The people calling themselves a "financial manager" has a great many alternative ways to rip off the client that are legal yet considered crooked. There is a fine line between what is or is not legitimate; most clients hardly noticing the difference. It is my contention that if most clients knew what was really happening with their money and how little effort it takes to manage your own money they would be outraged by it all.

As an active financial investor and trader, I have personally managed wealth for others over the years. My name is in *Who's Who of the World in Finance* so I assume I have room to speak out about the industry.

I sat in on a meeting after the death of a relative and listened to the financial advisor describe to the family what the situation had been and what the new strategy for the family money would be. He spoke in generalities and did not directly answer questions. More than $200,000 had been lost in investments by him and some of those involved a conflict of interest with the manager who was explaining everything. He had invested some family money in some of his friends and business partners ventures and lost it. His strategy sounded as though he was going to use the money left and supply the widow with enough to last over the next 10 years to her statistically expected death while siphoning as much off for himself as possible.

The deceased was a doctor who had found this manager at a fancy invitation-only dinner through a mailing list of potential clients fitting a particular financial profile. This is a very common marketing procedure by these managers and those who truly know the industry advise consumers never to attend one of these because they are so often just legal scammers. *Kiplinger* magazine, a publication with information that is trustworthy in my opinion, has written about similar events. This manager not only placed the deceased's money in terrible losing investments but also sold him an insurance policy that made no sense whatsoever. The insurance required him to pay about $500,000 in premiums over several years, the insurance would pay a few dollars less than $500,000. Why was this insurance sold to the deceased? The financial planner and the insurance agent realized huge commissions for selling the policy to the deceased. This planner talked the deceased, who was about 80 years old, into starting a charitable trust worth $500,000 to save on capital gains taxes from redeeming his prior investments. It was later found he would have paid much less tax on this than he thought he would save. Talking the deceased into selling his prior investments was a way to get the deceased to give the money to the "financial planner" for management. It was bothersome to hear this person talk about "behind the curtain fees" that the client never knows about. This planner was doing things like buying and selling stock in the deceased's family account on a daily basis regardless of profit or loss for the commission on it. It was clear his strategy was to siphon off any money that the client's money could muster.

Once it became clear that this financial planner was a con artist, my relative found another money manager at another promotional dinner. He seemed honest and nice so the money was transferred to him. One of the first things this money manager did was try to sell products to his new client. He was upfront that there was a commission but never said how much. He used tactics like "when the pool of money is full for this investment you can no longer invest in it." Close your eyes and try to imagine a financial entity – whose job relies on collecting money to invest, not taking money to invest on the premise that it would be too much money to invest. Is it making sense to you? I did not think so.

Another utterance this financial manager made was that he was going to take much of the money in the client account and turn it over to Ken Heebner, a well-known mutual fund manager, to manage. Wait a second! Why could I not just place my money with Ken Heebner and forget my financial manager and his fees? You mean now we not only have to pay your fees but Ken's as well? Sound reasonable? Not really.

This manager talked of having so many clients that he wanted to hire an institution to manage them for him. He would then only have to dot the i's and cross the t's on each account while raking in the fees. Does this sound like a guy who is carefully watching over your money?

Let us go back to the behind the curtain fee concept. David Jackson of SeekingAlpha.com points out that juicy, largely invisible fees are the primary reason Financial Manager accounts are Wall Street's most popular new trend.

The typical managed account includes several players, each of whom gets a piece of the action. At the helm is the primary salesperson—usually a broker or investment advisor who sells you on the idea - helps decide on asset allocation (such as stocks or bonds) and communicates with the sub-managers. Unfortunately, the *costs do not end with the main adviso*r. In a typical wrap account, a group of sub-advisors or mutual fund managers manage part of the wrap account's money. The primary advisor siphons off 0.5 percent to 1.2 percent a year of the assets in the account, while each sub-manager earns between 0.35 percent and 0.70 percent or more (bond managers earn less). In addition, there is generally a plan sponsor and a clearing and custody agent who takes another 0.15 to 1.0 percent. Investors with $300,000 or less will often pay as much as 2.7 percent a year when all the fees are added up. Even investors with several million or more will often pay over 1.25 and 2.5 percent.

Further, because stock-oriented funds and accounts typically pay the manager more than conservative bond-oriented funds, there is a built-in incentive for the managers to recommend a more aggressive allocation of assets (stocks or bonds), with far more stock funds than bond funds, even if that asset allocation is not appropriate.

Adding to the problems, most of these accounts are cookie cutter: once the asset allocation (stocks, bonds or cash) has been selected, the underlying funds are automatically bought. You cannot choose among the funds and if you decide to change your asset allocation, the change is made all at once, with new funds replacing the old ones. A better way - rebalancing or making changes gradually over several quarters - never happens with these accounts because that would be more work and less profit for the managers.

Advisors commonly claim that their managed accounts will give you access to the best, most successful money managers specially chosen by panels of consultants—access that you could not get if you just went shopping for a mutual fund through a discount broker. However, Yale University's Endowment Chief Investment Officer, David Swenson, disputes the idea that there are special consultants who can justly claim to be able to pick the best sub-managers and mutual funds. There [are] also more fees on top of existing fees." (*Responsible Investing*, June 2009)

The key is not to lose sight of the most important issue, which is: how much is this going to cost me, and what is going to be left over for me after my manager has taken his cut?

Investors should not worry that paying less for financial services will mean that they will miss the chance to get rich with some mythical brilliant investor. Neither private wealth managers, nor hedge fund managers, nor mutual fund managers have proven that they can do a consistently superior job managing your money. Passive investing in index funds with low fees is the best alternative for many investors. And all the evidence has shown that even in markets as tumultuous as 2008, a simple portfolio of low-cost stock and bond index funds, rebalanced periodically, will beat almost all active managers almost all of the time.

Pesky details.

Most investors have absolutely no idea how much money advisors earn from their investments. There is certainly nothing wrong with advisors being compensated for their work but the problem arises when there is a lack of transparency in the advisor/client relationship like "behind the curtain" fees. You should know exactly how much you are paying for the investments and services you receive. Only then can you make an informed decision on whether or not you are receiving a good value for your money.

I cannot tell you how many times people say to me, "Oh, I didn't pay my advisor anything. The insurance company paid him, not me."

Alternatively, I will hear, "Commission? What commission? I just bought a muni bond, not a stock." The problem with commissions is that you do not always see them. But trust me, there is no such thing as a free lunch. You are paying something, whether you realize it or not.

The way to save all the grief and rip off is to manage your own money.

IV.GOVERNMENT WORK

Chapter Eleven

GOVERNMENT MANAGEMENT

I considered my first job as real because I wore a suit to work each day. I had just earned my B.A. in the capital city where the state government was seated in a less than populous state. The capital was humming because state sales tax was just legislated and a completely new department in government was being developed.

I had heard that the State department was hiring anyone who walked in so I entered the Personnel department for the tax commission where a ton of young applicants was hired on the spot. A young African-American walked in while I was sitting there and asked the clerk if they were hiring. The clerk said that they were not hiring and would not be doing so any time soon. I had never seen such blatant discrimination in my life. I was shocked at such practice and in light of the civil rights movement having passed thought it odd that state government would do this kind of thing. As I thought back, I had never seen a black person in any of my schools or on the street before. I knew they were there but had never been associated with or seen any before.

As for my new job, sets of rules and procedures had to be developed along with a system for information to flow from department to department within the Tax Commission. There was this huge computer in a large room specially cooled with its own air conditioning, employees be damned.

There was a department within the state tax commission called Clearance, where all the guys were new, young, mostly part time and going to college. When taxpayers would call back, they always asked for "Clarence" instead, like Clarence the Clown worked there.

I was hired part time and the first day I wore a suit. That morning I was told to go help a fellow move a couple of desks. I was the person on the elevator moving a desk in a suit.

I suppose I could have accepted my position as a newbie desk mover in a suit but the department was new and I thought if I just kept coming to work in a suit I would soon be placed with the other people in suits. It worked. I was sat down and trained regarding the problems common to the tax returns coming into the Commission and how to take care of them. There were maybe 10 or 15 common problems and I soon learned the rules for taking care of them. Most of the problems concerned basic arithmetic and calling the taxpayer for clarification to resolve the problem. The information was then entered into a 360 IBM station and fed to the computer database basking in the air conditioning in another room.

Most of my fellow workers were fine people but there were a few strange ducks that always seemed to vie for attention. There was the fellow who got his job by working for the governor as his driver during the gubernatorial campaign. He happened to be a member of the same political party as the governor; the dominant party of the state. Of course, I was not a member of that party. I participated in a major presidential campaign of my own party at that time and this made us strange taxation bed fellows indeed. He was fat and hokey; he had a flat top and was always squirting some kind of breath spray into his mouth. He was from a small country town and came off like an ignorant country bumpkin with an "aw shucks" accent, about half of each word coming out of his nostrils. What I should have taken note of was that this person had the ear of the governor himself. Several of us in Clearance would go to lunch with each other and come back with beer breath. That may have been the first dumb thing I did in a job but not the last.

Working for a government agency is not like working for a for-profit organization. A government agency is there to keep track of things and to be sure everything is in order. If a member of the citizenry makes a mistake or does not comply with the rules and laws then we were there to make sure things were brought into line. A for-profit organization is there to develop new and devious ways to part the consumer from their hard-earned money by selling some product or service. The government agency is there to take money from the citizens to give them government services. The tax payer paid because it is the law and that makes people sometimes resentful. More than once, I called a taxpayer to clear things up with their return and they would hang up on me as though I was personally trying to take their money from them. Those folks just never formed the connection between their taxes and the paved highway, the schools built for their children to attend, the police to deal with crime or the firefighters there to put out their fires. It takes a few brain cells between the ears to make that connection apparently.

Once you are hired as full time by the government, it is very hard to fire you. There are specific ways of doing this but someone must want you gone very, very badly. In a for-profit situation, you can be fired for furrowing your brow at the wrong moment. Likewise you can lose a client at the blink of an eye.

These days you do have access to the wrongful termination laws but they usually do not take you very far. In a bureaucracy, you have to make someone mad enough they dig something up, point out incompetence or at least set things up so you look bad. It is sort of a process of demonization.

If there is a slow point in the work, it is ok to sit around and talk to each other. The bulk of the work at the tax commission was done just before the tax deadlines. One of the ideas behind government employment is jobs for people. Productivity is a much different animal than that of for-profit productivity. As long as things are organized and in line according to the rules, it is considered productive in government. In the private sector productivity is supposed to be ongoing, never at rest, always moving toward staving off the loss of a client or accumulating revenue and growth. Government work is revenue guaranteed depending on the economy. In my humble opinion the non-elected government employee only need fear the fellow employee out to get him for any reason whatsoever be it political or personal. Promotion in government depends more on whom you are able to impress with personal charm, wit, and talent, second. Note that

129

people are given promotions in any president's administration regardless of background and talent, based on how well they handle themselves. When we think back on presidential appointments there are numerous secretaries given promotions based on loyalty or reputation.

In the government agency, you are safe, barring another employee finding something that might look bad to the public or worst case scenario, revealed through the media.

When I was working at the tax commission, I had just graduated with my B.A. I had several friends who stayed in the same college town as I where I was also working in the state capital. One old friend of mine, Norm, was a Phi Beta Kappa, Dean's List, President of the Model United Nations meeting and every other achievement award at my school. He was smart and took a job with the Equal Employment Opportunity Commission (EEOP). This commission was new as the Civil Rights laws had just been passed. Norm and I would meet for drinks after work and talk the politics of the day. One thing I noticed was that whatever and wherever I had a job there were only white males there. I thought nothing of it. When I husked corn as a kid there were only white kids working for DeKalb. When I worked on construction jobs scooping concrete in the summer there were only white people working around me. I saw my first black person when my parents and I traveled to the South. I had heard that the town I lived in had a "black section," although I was not sure where it was or if it even existed.

There were no black people working in the tax commission until later. There was one fellow who worked with Norm in the EEOC who had some sort of Spanish surname but he was the only non-white with the exception of the Director who was African-American. The tax commission did hire women but none worked in my department and I suspect it was because it was considered work you do with your brain. There were clerks who were women on a sort of conveyer belt where the raw tax returns came in and they opened the envelopes then sent them to the next level where the information was entered into a database on a primitive mainframe with terminals to update taxpayer information.

Those of us in the Clearance section knew we were special because we had our own code to get into the terminal and change or add taxpayer information. This was a powerful position.

Norm and I were talking about our new lives after graduation from college. Here we were with no homework at night. There was a paycheck involved. It took some getting used to.

The civil rights movement was still in full force at that time, people were still being discriminated against because of their skin, and of course, they still are.

Norm brought a new person into our after work meeting scene who was the Director of the EEOC and so began the first real relationship I had experienced with a black person. His name was Dennis and we were both aware that there were differences between our life experiences but I was not knowledgeable what the details might be, exactly. That became the basis for our conversations and relationship for some time. The three of us would get together and loosen up with drinks then openly discuss our understanding of what it must have been like to grow up as the other. Dennis was keenly intelligent, having graduated with a Master's and Law degree.

Over time we slowly pried open the parts of ourselves not normally opened by such divergent racial experience. He thought me a "cross bearing" white man bearing the cross for wrongdoing by the white man to the black man as in slavery and other oppressive cultural realities by my fellow whites.

I must admit, seeing on television the southern police riots, the sicking of dogs on old people and spraying water from fire hydrants at people, knocking them into trees and blowing eardrums out, made me feel rather odd about white people. Then there was President Kennedy, who federalized the Alabama State Militia to stand up to Governor George Wallace at the school entry so that a black child could enter and become educated.

Dennis was one of 10 children, half of whom landed in the state penitentiary. He somehow had battled the odds and not only became a straight "A" student but was able to fend off the peer pressure to fail and drop out of school. He entered Harvard on a scholarship and graduated with a law degree at the top of his class. He took the advice of President Kennedy to find a career in public service rather than as a corporate lawyer. As the Director of the

EEOC, he was driven to find what it was in the white heart that allowed whites to see the black person as less than admirable.

I think we concluded that in certain cultures the white man thought of the black man as more primitive and animal in nature. The lower the status of the white man, the more likely he'd need a lackey or someone lower in stature to look down on in order to make himself feel superior. So the lower the class and the lower the education the more likely racism would raise its ugly head. Much research has been done on this and it seems to hold true in the socio-scientific world.

I could not relate to Dennis's life experience, but I understood he had to work a lot harder, be a lot more motivated and nderstand the system better because he was black. My rise in life was much easier, easier to retain, and we were both clear on that.

Meanwhile, the newly elected governor needed to make a move to gain the black vote. The two major cities had large populations of potential black voters thanks to the new "right to vote" law. The Governor saw the perfect move in appointing Dennis as the Director of the State Division of Motor Vehicles. This was huge! Dennis was going to be the first black man ever appointed to a directorship of this state division in history.

Norm, Dennis and I were soon making plans for his rise in the political system. His next move had to be the right one and that would be the Senate or the governorship itself. Preparations had to be made, strategy and connections planned.

Dennis took his directorship to heart wanting to be fresh and efficient. What he found was the old guard, the unelected employees who had been running the division for years, avoiding change, freshness and efficiency. Dennis was probably correct in his perception of the old hierarchy resenting his being their boss. After all, he was black and they were old white people. One Friday after work, we gathered at the drinking hole and he said he had a plan to handle the situation. He was going to call a meeting and tell those at the top of the organization to either hand him their resignation or convince him why they should be allowed to stay. This would let them know who was now in charge.

"Holy crap!" were the words out of my mouth. I had seen how it works in a bureaucracy. They would find a way to get rid of him, somehow, someway.

"If you do that, they will give you the axe." I told him, feeling the stress of what he was about to do and what would happen. I knew this is what happens in government. You can get away with murder but unless someone wants you gone, you get to keep your job. However, if someone wants you gone and is willing to go through the effort, you can be canned for having stolen a candy bar as a child. You can be fired for jaywalking in an alley.

Dennis occasionally left our "after work" meetings inebriated. I sometimes wondered how he would drive. In that day, people knew how to drink, never thinking twice before getting into a car to drive home.

My new wife and I took a vacation to California and fell in love with it. We agreed to move there as soon as the weather permitted. That would be a few months later. Norm asked me if I would take a job at the EEOC, clearly a move by Norm and Dennis to keep me with them. We were sort of a rat pack by then. I told him that no, thanks for the offer but we are on our way to the land of sun and sky.

During one of our after work meetings, Dennis said that he needed help running the Division of Motor Vehicles. He offered me the Chief of Staff position reporting to him. I was flabbergasted! He said he needed me to become the person who would keep people aware that he wanted this to be an efficient and disciplined organization. What an offer that was! I told him I would think about it. Upon our next meeting, I told him I was going to California and could not accept. It was one of those forks in the road of life that had I taken might have taken me with him to the Senate, which he planned to run for in the near future. I would have carved a life out of politics and power but I had to go to California.

We proceeded to move to California and came back the next chance we had to visit old friends. Norm met with me at the old watering hole.

"Where is Dennis?" I asked Norm.

"People at the DMV dug up an old "Driving While Intoxicated" charge that Dennis had. The Governor fired him."

135

I was devastated, but not surprised. Norm's wife said, "Dennis sat right there," pointing to the chair I usually sat in. "He said you told him he would get the axe if he tried to clean things up." She repeated that several times and it felt just as chilling to me each time she said it. There was this feeling that a great character was lost to pettiness of bureaucrats and politics. The brightness of his plans and my coming within a hair of being a part of that excitement just made me depressed and angry at the whole process. In a bureaucracy as long as you drag yourself in and things are done efficiently you have a job. However, it is a highly political and edgy situation. People will find a way to get rid of you if you make waves of any kind. The element to keep in mind is, should you find yourself working for the government, if you are a human, you most likely have something in your background that can get you fired. I do not know where Norm or Dennis are today.

End

www.ingramcontent.com/pod-product-compliance
Lightning Source LLC
Chambersburg PA
CBHW060045210326
41520CB00009B/1276